**British History in Per:**
General Editor: Jeremy Black

PUBLISHED TITLES

(List continued overleaf)

Further titles are in preparation

Please note that a sister series, *Social History in Perspective*, is now available. It covers the key topics in social, cultural and religious history.

**British History in Perspective**
Series Standing Order ISBN 0–333–69331–0

You can receive future titles in this series as they are published by placing a standing order. Please contact your bookseller or, in case of difficulty, write to us at the address below with your name and address, the title of the series and the ISBN quoted above.

Customer Services Department, Macmillan Distribution Ltd
Houndmills, Basingstoke, Hampshire RG21 6XS, England

# Scotland in the Nineteenth Century

John F. McCaffrey

First published in Great Britain 1998 by
**MACMILLAN PRESS LTD**
Houndmills, Basingstoke, Hampshire RG21 6XS and London
Companies and representatives throughout the world

A catalogue record for this book is available from the British Library.

ISBN 0–333–58752–9 hardcover
ISBN 0–333–58753–7 paperback

---

First published in the United States of America 1998 by
**ST. MARTIN'S PRESS, INC.,**
Scholarly and Reference Division,
175 Fifth Avenue, New York, N.Y. 10010

ISBN 0–312–21124–4

Library of Congress Cataloging-in-Publication Data
McCaffrey, John.
Scotland in the nineteenth century / John McCaffrey.
p.   cm. — (British history in perspective)
Includes bibliographical references and index.
ISBN 0–312–21124–4 (cloth)
1. Scotland—History—19th century.   I. Title.   II. Series.
DA815.M377  1998
941.1081—dc21                                              97–37239
                                                                CIP

This book is printed on paper suitable for recycling and made from fully managed and sustained forest sources.

10   9   8   7   6   5   4   3   2   1
07   06   05   04   03   02   01   00   99   98

Printed in Hong Kong

# CONTENTS

# PREFACE

In this book I have tried to show how Scotland became a different kind of society in the nineteenth century, developing many of the features which still influence the lives of its inhabitants today. As it became industrialised and urbanised like its larger neighbour England, to whom it had been joined in a legislative union in 1707, it became a more integral part of the United Kingdom. Despite the rapidity of these changes, however, and the resulting tendencies to uniformity, Scotland retained a distinctive identity while, at the same time, reinforcing its British links in its cultural and institutional adaptations to these modern pressures. Its history is, therefore, more than a regional variation of the social and economic trends which were affecting Britain and Europe at this time. Much of its commercial expansion was fostered by an outlook, already well established by 1800, which was ready to adjust and experiment. Much of that outlook was itself due to the desire for commercial progress, which again can be traced back to before 1700. Which was the prime mover in this process will probably never be satisfactorily decided by historians. What is clear is that change depended on much more than economic forces, although these are an important part of the story. It also depended on pre-existing beliefs and institutions which embodied values and practices suited to a highly localised country lacking any tradition of strong central government. As political participation widened, what is striking in nineteenth-century Scotland is how the arguments about the way it should adapt to change were expressed in an almost total commitment to the Liberal party. Partly this was due to its desire to become an ever closer part of those progressive forces which were expanding British power, but partly, too, it was because it saw its role in Britain expressed in its response to that particular timing and blend of economic and social changes which had affected it. In writing this book I have drawn on the enormous body of work on Scotland which has appeared over the past 30 years and I have tried to acknowledge this wherever possible. My other debts are to the many students whose questions have constantly challenged my views on the history of Scotland. More specifically, I thank Professor Archie Duncan for his encouragement over the years. I owe a great deal especially to my former colleague, John Gilfillan, for much insight and discussion, the value of which can never be truly measured. I am grateful to Dr Irene Maver for having commented on the typescript. The map is reproduced from Professor Bruce Lenman's *An Economic History of Modern Scotland*, by kind permission of the author. Most of all, I have to thank my wife Caroline, not least for her preference for plain English, and to her I dedicate this book.

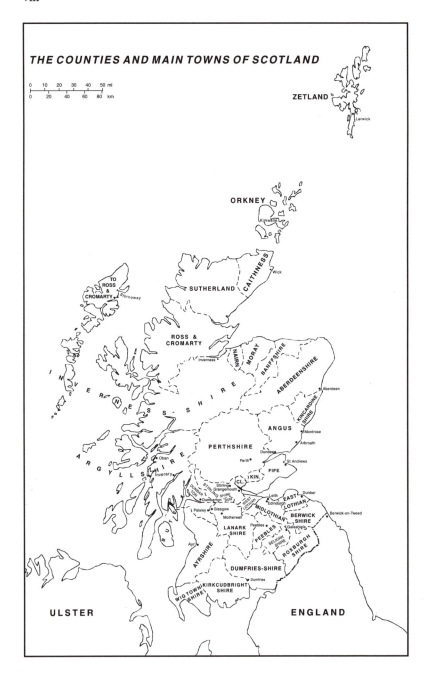

### THE COUNTIES AND MAIN TOWNS OF SCOTLAND

0  10  20  30  40  50 ml

0   20   40   60   80 km

ZETLAND

Lerwick

ORKNEY

Kirkwall

CAITHNESS

Wick

SUTHERLAND

TO ROSS & CROMARTY

Stornoway

ROSS & CROMARTY

Inverness

NAIRN

MORAY

BANFFSHIRE

ABERDEENSHIRE

Aberdeen

I N V E R N E S S - S H I R E

KINCARDINE SHIRE

ANGUS

Montrose

Arbroath

A R G Y L L S H I R E

PERTHSHIRE

Dundee

Oban

Inverary

Perth

FIFE

St Andrews

Stirling

STIRLING SHIRE

Grangemouth

CL.

KIN.

DUNBAR TON

WEST LOTHIAN

Dumbarton

DUN.

Leith

Edinburgh

EAST LOTHIAN

Dunbar

Glasgow

MIDLOTHIAN

Paisley

BERWICK SHIRE

Berwick-on-Tweed

Motherwell

LANARK SHIRE

Peebles

PEEBLES

Galashiels

SELKIRK SHIRE

ROXBURGH SHIRE

B U T E

Ayr

AYRSHIRE

DUMFRIES-SHIRE

Dumfries

WIGTOWN SHIRE

KIRKCUDBRIGHT SHIRE

ULSTER

ENGLAND

# 1

# A SOCIETY IN TRANSITION: 1800–32

Scotland was becoming a new sort of society in 1800. Its population was increasing rapidly and continued to do so right up to 1914 (see Table 1.1). Constant expansion like this, even when offset by emigration (which was particularly heavy in the 1850s, 1880s and 1900s) put great strain on the country's institutions and customary attitudes. At the same time it was also becoming an increasingly urbanised society (Table 1.2). These were relatively recent developments. England at this time was experiencing even higher rates of population growth, but it had had longer to adjust to the economic and social forces which were causing such changes. The impact was more sudden in Scotland which, in a list of 16 urbanised societies in Europe (measured by the proportion of their population in towns of 10 000 and above), had advanced from seventh place in 1750 to fourth in 1800, and lay second only to England and Wales by 1850.[1] Even if most of its inhabitants in 1800 were not yet town dwellers, a dynamic commercial sector was becoming

*Table 1.1   Population.*

| Year | Total | Percentage increase | Year | Total | Percentage increase |
|------|-------|---------------------|------|-------|---------------------|
| 1801 | 1 608 420 |        | 1861 | 3 062 294 | (6.0) |
| 1811 | 1 805 864 | (12.4) | 1871 | 3 360 018 | (9.7) |
| 1821 | 2 091 521 | (15.8) | 1881 | 3 735 573 | (11.2) |
| 1831 | 2 364 386 | (13.0) | 1891 | 4 025 647 | (7.8) |
| 1841 | 2 620 184 | (10.8) | 1901 | 4 472 103 | (11.1) |
| 1851 | 2 888 742 | (10.2) | 1911 | 4 760 904 | (6.5) |

*Source*: J. G. Kyd, *Scottish Population Statistics* (Scottish History Society, 3rd series, vol. XLIV, Edinburgh, 1952), pp. xvii, xx.

1

*Table 1.2    Urban growth.*

| Year | Percentage in towns of 5000 and over | Year | Percentage in towns of 5000 and over |
|------|------|------|------|
| 1801 | 21   | 1861 | 39.4 |
| 1811 | 24   | 1871 | 44.4 |
| 1821 | 27.5 | 1881 | 48.9 |
| 1831 | 31.2 | 1891 | 53.5 |
| 1841 | 32.7 | 1901 | 57.6 |
| 1851 | 35.9 | 1911 | 58.6 |

*Source*: M. W. Flinn, *Scottish Population History from the 17th Century to the 1930s* (Cambridge, 1977), p. 313.

increasingly influential in directing their lives and fortunes. By the 1850s the balance had tilted definitely now to the urban, the Registrar-General for Scotland estimating in 1861 that only 36 per cent of the population remained in rural surroundings with another 12 per cent in small villages, leaving 52 per cent in true towns of over 2000 inhabitants.

All the major cities were expanding, the new textile and commercial centres on the Clyde remarkably so. Between 1801 and 1841, Glasgow went from 77 000 to 275 000, Edinburgh from 83 000 to 166 000, Aberdeen (which also had a large textile component) from 27 600 to 63 000 and Dundee from 26 000 to 63 000. In the same period, Paisley leapt from 25 000 to 48 000 (60 000 if all the surrounding districts in the Abbey parish are included) and Greenock from 17 000 to 36 000. Older regional centres such as Perth, Ayr or Dumfries also increased steadily. The growth of parishes made up mainly of textile villages was equally dramatic and, given their more limited resources, perhaps more traumatic. In Neilston in Renfrewshire (where the *Old Statistical Account*[2] recorded that since the growth of cotton mills, print and bleachfields, 'the mode of precisely ascertaining the number of inhabitants for any given time beyond a few months, is but uncertain') the estimated 2300 of 1791 had jumped to 8000 by 1831. As cloth printing and dyeworks expanded along the river Leven in Dunbartonshire, the population of Bonhill parish doubled from 3800 in 1821 to 7600 by 1851. Even a traditional small town such as Alva, nestling at the foot of the Ochils, quickly went from 1300 in 1831 to 3200 in 1851 once a new woollen mill was established there. Despite the spectacular growth of Glasgow, Scotland was becoming a country of medium and small towns, and this pattern continued during the next large expansion in coal, iron and engineering, which began in the 1830s. Up to 1821, Edinburgh had matched Glasgow for size. Thereafter, Glasgow drew away and, by 1851, with some 12 per cent of the Scottish population, it contained as many people as the next three largest cities (Edinburgh, Dundee and Aberdeen) put together – but it remained exceptional, more like the great industrial cities of England than the other Scottish conurbations. By mid-century England had 63 towns above the 20 000 population level: Scotland had only nine, and of these only four were above the 50 000 size, compared with 24 in England. The majority of Scottish towns had populations of under 20 000 with the great bulk of these below 10 000. Much of the initial Scottish urban experience, therefore, despite the lurid pictures so often drawn by historians using statistics from Glasgow and Edinburgh, was of small town society, intensely localised and given great diversity by the country's highly contrasting topographies.

The shape of society was being altered, too, with the balance increasingly tilting towards the narrow central belt lying between the Clyde and the Forth and the Tay (Table 1.3). These census snapshots show the results of constant short-term movements first to the small towns, and then on to the larger cities where there might be opportunity for work. In the far north and north-east, population drifted to Aberdeen and the towns in its vicinity along the Moray Firth or south down to Montrose or Arbroath. In the districts above the Tay, the direction was to Perth and Dundee. Edinburgh had traditionally been a magnet for all areas around the Forth and the south-east. In the west, by 1851 all roads were leading to Glasgow and the industrial towns surrounding it. Much of the migration from the nearer western Highlands came to this Clyde region. In the further north and western Highlands and Islands, the trend was to move out of Scotland altogether.[3] These population movements brought people from different regional cultures to live in close proximity, forcing them into the difficult process of making new accommodations and adjustments. Long before migration from Ireland began to have an effect on the make-up of Scotland's population, this was already becoming a society of 'new' Scots, cut off from their traditional historical links, in a very real sense 'immigrants' in a new world of economic growth, transoceanic markets and constantly changing technology.

Traditionally, of course, there always had been some movement: of tradesmen to where work was available, of cottars and small tenants to new locations or of Highlanders migrating seasonally to the Lowlands in order to supplement crofting incomes. In the early nineteenth

*Table 1.3    Population distribution: totals
(with percentage in each region in brackets).*

| Region | 1801 | 1831 | 1851 | 1881 | 1901 |
|---|---|---|---|---|---|
| Crofting | 302 817 | 388 876 | 395 540 | 369 453 | 352 371 |
| | (18.8) | (16.4) | (13.7) | (9.9) | (7.9) |
| North-East | 220 712 | 301 277 | 349 716 | 419 433 | 460 941 |
| | (13.7) | (12.7) | (12.1) | (11.2) | (10.3) |
| **North total** | **523 529** | **690 153** | **745 256** | **788 886** | **813 312** |
| | **(32.5)** | **(29.2)** | **(25.8)** | **(21.1)** | **(18.2)** |
| Forth-Tay | 557 214 | 785 814 | 927 538 | 1 183 294 | 1 400 675 |
| | (34.6) | (33.2) | (32.1) | (31.7) | (31.3) |
| Greater | 342 901 | 642 679 | 942 829 | 1 478 295 | 1 995 427 |
| Clyde | (21.3) | (27.2) | (32.6) | (39.6) | (44.6) |
| **Central total** | **900 115** | **1 428 493** | **1 870 367** | **2 661 589** | **3 396 102** |
| | **(55.9)** | **(60.4)** | **(64.7)** | **(71.3)** | **(75.9)** |
| Eastern | 78 050 | 95 122 | 108 486 | 128 220 | 118 050 |
| Borders | (4.9) | (4.0) | (3.8) | (3.4) | (2.6) |
| Western | 106 726 | 150 618 | 164 633 | 156 878 | 144 639 |
| Borders | (6.6) | (6.4) | (5.7) | (4.2) | (3.2) |
| **South total** | **184 776** | **245 740** | **273 119** | **285 098** | **262 689** |
| | **(11.5)** | **(10.4)** | **(9.5)** | **(7.6)** | **(5.9)** |

*Source*: R. H. Osborne, 'The movements of people in Scotland, 1851–1951',
*Scottish Studies*, 2 (1958), p. 3.
Crofting: Argyll, Inverness, Ross & Cromarty, Sutherland, Caithness, Orkney,
Shetland.
North-East: Aberdeen, Kincardine, Banff, Moray, Nairn.
Forth–Tay: Angus, Perth, Fife, Clackmannan, Kinross, Stirling, East-, West-
and Mid-Lothian.
Greater Clyde: Lanark, Renfrew, Dunbarton, Ayrshire, Bute.
Eastern Borders: Berwick, Roxburgh, Selkirk, Peebles
Western Borders: Dumfries, Kirkcudbright, Wigtown.

century, however, such mobility became an increasing and more constant feature in people's lives. Anyone making even a cursory examination of census schedules in the nineteenth century will be struck by the
different birthplaces of the children in the same families. This was particularly so with certain groups such as coalminers. One observer liken-
ed them to shoals of herring. Landless labourers, like Alexander
Somerville in the Lammermoors, now regularly moved back and forth,
working at various hard labouring tasks in the towns and countryside of
the Lothians. In Ettrick parish in Selkirkshire, it was recorded in 1832
that less than half the adults were natives. Cotton spinners in Glasgow

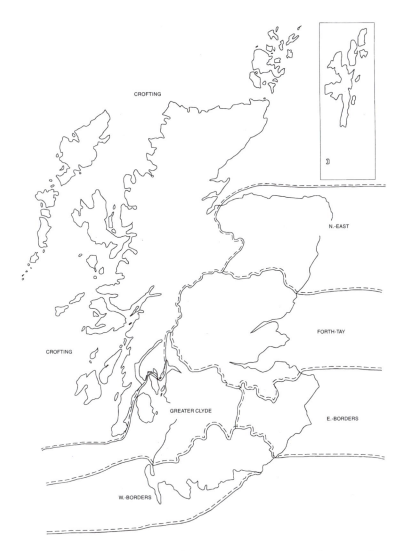

CROFTING

N.-EAST

FORTH-TAY

CROFTING

GREATER CLYDE

E.-BORDERS

W.-BORDERS

were able to cite conditions and wages in American textile towns from first-hand knowledge to the Factory Inquiry Commissioners in 1833. Alexander Somerville's father, born in the Ochils, moved to Alloa to work as a carter, and then to Ayton in Berwickshire near the English border as an agricultural labourer, where he married. Thereafter his children were born at various farms in Berwickshire and East Lothian.

One of Alexander's brothers became a cooper at Leith, another a for-
ester in Yorkshire, while he and another brother eventually became
soldiers. Many ordinary people who did not leave autobiographies
must have been like a Mormon family whose records have survived.
The mother, born in Stromness, Orkney, married a weaver in
Edinburgh. They then moved to Pollokshaws, at that time a village on
the outskirts of Glasgow. Widowed, she returned to Edinburgh and
married a collier in Tranent who had been born in Edinburgh, who
then worked variously as a draper and a colliery clerk after their marriage in a succession of small Lanarkshire towns such as Whifflet and
Wishaw before emigrating to the United States in search of a better life.[4]

Emigration was another element in this changing social picture, constantly widening people's horizons and sharpening their perceptions
while acting as a safety valve to pressure at home. This, too, had always
been a feature of Scottish society, but had caused increasing concern in
the later eighteenth century when large numbers, particularly from the
Highlands, had gone first to the American Colonies and then to
Canada. After 1815 increasing numbers of Lowlanders also began to
leave for North America, particularly in depressed years such as 1818,
1828 or 1832, with a marked rise in the early 1840s. In addition, there
had always been a significant number who tried their fortune in
England. The rough estimates available suggest that about 51 000 emigrants in all left Scotland in the 1830s, rising to 59 000 in the 1840s and
154 000 in the 1850s, reflecting the difficult economic conditions of
these years. The figures for the 1840s and 1850s would also include
many Irish migrants to Scotland who left for America once they had
made enough money. Official statistics available from the 1850s onwards (Table 1.4) show that Scotland lost a staggering 30 per cent of its
natural increase because of emigration in the second half of the nineteenth century, much of it overseas – especially to the United States – so
it is likely that the outward flow was also significant in the first half.

Table 1.4   *Net Emigration 1861–1911.*

| 1861–1911: | Natural Population increase | |
|---|---|---|
| | (births over deaths) | 2 433 756 |
| | Actual Population increase | 1 698 610 |
| | Net migration loss | 735 146 |
| | (= 30.2 per cent of natural increase) | |

*Source*: Kyd, *Scottish Population Statistics*, pp. xix–xxi.

Movement out of the country at these levels must represent some judgement on contemporary society as well as a desire for better opportunities, perhaps some criticism of a social structure which limited the possibility of landholding, or frustration at the rigidities imposed by the newer individualistic economics operating within a still hierarchical society. Whatever it was, at these levels it was becoming part of the consciousness of an increasing number of families, giving other dimensions to their everyday experiences through their links with the emigrants. The movement of some of these migrants back to Scotland, plus the wide coverage given to emigration in the popular press and in pamphlets, ensured that it would remain so.[5]

The new social mixtures were most obvious in the industrial Lowlands, drawing permanent migrants in from the Gaelic areas of Scotland and from the north and north-west of Ireland. Gaelic places of worship had already sprung up by 1800 in all the major Lowland towns from Aberdeen down to Perth, Dundee, Edinburgh, Glasgow, Paisley and Greenock.[6] Irish migrants, from an even larger pool (Ireland's population in 1800 was some five million compared with about 300 000 in the Scottish highlands), soon began to outstrip them (Table 1.5). To the traditional Irish harvesters were added permanent settlers, mainly from Ulster, who became well represented in the cotton-spinning factories, in handloom weaving, and in all the heavy labouring (and often skilful) work of canal, road, railway, pier and harbour building of this time. By the 1830s the total number of Irish-born had climbed to about 107 000, located mainly in the central and southwestern areas of Scotland. If their children born in Scotland are included, their numbers would be higher, especially in magnet areas such as Glasgow where

*Table 1.5    Irish-born (with percentage of total population in brackets).*

| Year | Number |
|------|--------|
| 1841 | 126 321 (4.8) |
| 1851 | 207 367 (7.2) |
| 1861 | 204 083 (6.7) |
| 1871 | 207 770 (6.2) |
| 1881 | 218 745 (5.9) |
| 1891 | 194 807 (4.8) |
| 1901 | 205 064 (4.6) |
| 1911 | 174 715 (3.7) |

Precise figures are available only from 1841, when information on place of birth was included in the Census.

they probably made up about 25 per cent of the population by the 1830s. The great majority (estimates vary from three-quarters to two-thirds) were Roman Catholics. Visible signs of this were the permanent Roman Catholic chapels already erected in Paisley, Dumfries, Edinburgh, Greenock and Glasgow by 1816, and the increase in the overall numbers of Roman Catholics in Scotland from 30 000 in 1800 to 70 000 in 1827 and 146 000 by 1851. In a country so deeply moulded by the Reformation, their growth in the new urban areas was bound to alter the nature of Scottish society profoundly.[7] The small indigenous Catholic community itself had to struggle to adjust to the demands made by these new numbers. Scottish priests like Andrew Scott (later bishop of the Western District) found himself at odds with a vociferous minority among the Irish Catholics in the 1820s because of their support for radical O'Connellite politics. The first holding of an 'Orange Walk' in Glasgow in 1821 by the minority of Protestant Irish settlers did little to help matters. Not all reactions were hostile. A Catholic Schools Society was established in Glasgow in 1817 (following one in Paisley in 1816) by a group of leading merchants, in which a committee, half Catholic and half Protestant, appointed Catholic teachers using the Protestant version of the Bible, as a way of meeting the educational needs of these migrants and helping them to integrate into urban society.[8]

It should be remembered, however, that most of those experiencing the problems of adjustment in the burgeoning urban centres were native Scots. This can be seen in one of the fastest growing towns in Scotland in this period, Paisley. Of its 5760 households in the early 1820s, 669 (11.6 per cent) had been born in highland counties (mainly Argyll and Bute), and 603 (10.5 per cent) in Ireland, but 2600 (45.1 per cent) came from other counties in Scotland (mainly the rest of Renfrewshire, Ayrshire and Lanarkshire). A shrewd observer of the contemporary scene in the west of Scotland, John Tait (editor of the radical newspaper, the *Liberator*), estimated in the early 1830s that natives of Glasgow made up only one-fifth of its population: the rest were one-fifth Highlanders, one-fifth Irish and two fifths incomers from the surrounding Lowlands.[9] Even if the proportions were inexact, his general impressions were correct. By 1851, when the Census recorded places of birth, it showed that 53 per cent of the inhabitants of the ten principal towns in Scotland were incomers. Again, as might be expected, chief among these was Glasgow, nearly 56 per cent of whose inhabitants in that year had been born outside of the city. Of these, some 18 per cent had been born in Ireland, but the majority had been born elsewhere in Scotland:

16.9 per cent in the surrounding counties, 9.7 per cent in the eastern Lowlands and 5.2 per cent in the Highlands. It was a pattern repeated in every other industrial area and not until the 1870s did incomers cease to be the predominant element. Even in more stable environments such as the city of Perth, 40 per cent of its inhabitants in 1851 had been born elsewhere, having come into the city mainly from the surrounding county and the rest of Scotland.

The cause of all this social flux was the increasing specialisation of the country's economy, particularly its agriculture. Improvements which had transformed farming in the south-east by the 1790s increasingly spread to become the norm in other areas after 1800. It has been estimated that between 1750 and 1825 there had been a 40 per cent increase in the total area farmed in Scotland and a 100 per cent increase in productivity.[10] This wrought changes in rural society as profound as those caused by the new machinery in manufacturing areas. Although patterns varied according to local circumstances, the general effect of the new system of enclosures, scientific crop and stock management, long leases and consolidated farms had been to turn some of the former joint occupiers into individual tenants and the rest (the great majority) into landless labourers, whose opportunities to remain on the land diminished with the need to balance employment with productivity. This resulted in a highly specialised and regional pattern in which labour requirements were carefully tailored to suit local conditions, preventing the creation of a large underemployed and potentially resentful residue. In the south-east, with its large farms and emphasis on arable, this division of employers and employees was at its most absolute. There the skilled agricultural labourers, or 'hinds', were employed on yearly or half-yearly contracts which gave them security, a cottage and part payment of their wages in kind as a hedge against inflation. Despite their loss of past status, such farm servants found themselves more cushioned than either those above or those below them when prices began to tumble after the end of the French Wars in 1815. In the more pastoral south-west with its specialised dairying, skilled labour could still be obtained from within the smaller family farms of that region. In the carses between the Forth and Angus, farm servants could be drawn from the small villages and cottages of the region, with single workers being housed in bothies. In the far north-east in Aberdeenshire and Banffshire, the drive to maximise holdings was offset by the need to maintain a number of small crofts from which the supply of skilled ploughmen could be obtained. In the regions outside of the south-east, therefore, some of those who supplied the skilled labour for the large farms always had a hope, no matter how slim, of one day getting back to occupancy of the land in smaller tenancies or crofts. However, the growing surplus who could not thus be accommodated at the half-yearly hiring fairs, or the farm servants who on marriage failed to get a cottage or a croft, or a place in a family farm, increasingly drifted to the less certain opportunities being opened up in urban manufacturing areas.

In such ways, this clearance of the small tenants of the former ferm touns to make way for a more efficient, modern agricultural system in the lowlands was less glaring than was the case in Highland crofting areas. However, there must have been the same resentments as large numbers had their historic ties with the land severed and replaced with a more impersonal commercial relationship. For those who remained, life was less certain and what security there was had been won at the cost of more intensive working practices. But, unlike Highland experience, change had occurred at different times in the Lowlands, first in the south east, and then spreading to the western and northeastern portions as these began to specialise in dairy and beef products for their growing industrial hinterlands. Opposition could be subsumed in the pride which skilled ploughmen and farm servants could take in being essential elements in their sector's success in output and quality. The continuity of traditions for those who remained, of diet, festival and rural amusements, of the independence which could be exercised at hiring fairs of turning down masters with a bad reputation, all these also helped. There were never any great groups of former tenants or cottars sharing one common experience which might have been welded into more outright forms of resistance. There were always the alternative opportunities, and perhaps even more interesting environments, developing in nearby local towns as stepping stones to larger cities. Familiarity with the large amount of manufacturing already carried out in rural areas, such as weaving, metalwork or milling, would make it easier for them to make the transition.

Strong regional identities remained, making it difficult to speak of a uniform Scottish historical experience in these changes, the sharp contrasts in topography between the various areas of the country reinforcing these new social patterns. Until better communication by roads or steamship became more generally available by 1830, distance was always a barrier. Dialect reinforced differences everywhere. It took Alexander Somerville time to get to grips with the Ayrshire dialect when he first came across a book of Burns' poems in the east of Scotland about 1822. Despite occasional lamentations that the old local culture was decaying, a strong tradition of music and ballads remained, and the continuance of instrumental bands and songmaking in the new industrial environments proved its persistence. Despite the thinning of the agricultural population as a result of such modernisation and its consequent overshadowing by the urban sector, the land still retained its importance economically, socially and psychologically in Scottish society.[11] Right through to the middle years of Victoria's reign it remained highly profitable. The setbacks after the return to peacetime conditions in 1815 were being overcome by the 1830s. The same is true of Highland Scotland. Its crofters and cottars remained in miserable conditions, but large estates continued to yield both high profits and pleasure when let by new commercial buyers for sheep or sport. Land-holding continued to confer political influence at both the national and local government level until the later nineteenth century. The 1832 Reform Act, by enabling tenants to vote and thus become liable to pressure from above at the open polling, added to landlord influence. Traditional rural forms of government were for long the model on which nineteenth-century administrative reforms were based. The continuing influence of the parish in education and social welfare, of the Commissioners of Supply in policing, and in road and bridge provision are typical examples. This was combined with social status. Successful merchants and manufacturers in Victorian Scotland seldom took their rewards in city life and pursuits, the favoured route more often being the acquisition of a landed estate. In a more general psychological sense, the countryside continued to exert a deep influence on the Scottish outlook. Its social and economic contrasts provided many of the radicals of the period with their agenda for reform. Others saw it as a haven of historical reassurance, in contrast to the increasing experience of congested towns and industrial villages, of noise and steam and heaps of industrial spoil. The popularity of painters such as John and Tom Faed or Sam Bough continued to prove this. At an everyday level, the growing numbers who came to live in the industrial areas were not cut off entirely from the soil. Their towns were usually small and easily traversed, their streets ending abruptly in sudden access to the surrounding fields. The prose and verse of Janet Hamilton, the poetess of industrial Lanarkshire in the 1850s, express the juxtaposition, and some of the consequent bewilderment, poignantly.

Attempts to extend the economic basis of the Highlands in accordance with the maxims of economic liberalism led to less reconcilable experiences in that region.[12] Modern historiography shows that it is wrong to treat 'the Highlands' as if it were a single undifferentiated area, or to discuss it always in terms of 'a problem'. In southern Argyll and in the eastern parts of the Highlands from easter Ross down to southern Perthshire, some balance between the newer agriculture and the region's resources was achieved. Seasonal migration to lowland farms or towns was easier because they were closer at hand: thus population levels were more evenly matched with alternatives. From Appin northwards and west to the outer Hebrides, however, landlords' decisions on how their estates should be developed had produced a more dependent and disorientated society by 1800. It is true that clan chiefs were subject to forces outwith their control. In general, the terrain and the cultural context made their room for manoeuvre narrower. However, decisions as to land use operated only one way throughout this region, and the creation of crofting communities or the introduction of sheep were choices made solely by the proprietors. Contrary to popular myth, population was growing more slowly in the western Highlands than in Scotland as a whole. The problem was that the resource base was expanding even more slowly and its main planks – cattle, fishing, kelp or alternatives such as distilling and quarrying – were too narrow to allow for the rapid change that most clan chiefs favoured. Some commentators advocated a thinning of the population while paying some attention to the social needs of the region through long-term investment. Here proprietors were caught up in the giddy atmosphere of the time. Whatever effort they might have been willing to make to achieve change from within was swept aside by the greater temptations to profit which the French wars had opened up. A large tenantry, for instance, enabled proprietors to raise companies of fencibles for the army. To burn the tons of seaweed thrown up on the western shores to produce kelp – providing essential chemicals just at the time when British industrial demand for them was growing and when alternative supplies were being blocked by Napoleon – also required manpower which could be cheaply retained and maintained. Crofting tenancies based largely on potato culture (the vast majority economically unviable at well under £10 rentals) kept people at home safe from the lure of America. Such schemes appeared to provide a solution to the financial and social challenges involved in managing Highland estates. Up to 1815, the profits available from war-time demand for cattle and kelp (in the Hebrides proprietors were estimated to be making up to £70 000 per annum from kelp alone) blinded proprietors to the exiguous basis of the structure that they had created. Expectations of higher incomes had encouraged many proprietors to incur long-term debts on rebuilding schemes and improved lifestyles. In spite of vast increases in rentals, the Clanranald estate had accumulated debts of over £100 000 by 1812 and the Seaforth estate debts of over £205 000 by 1815. These were only the more spectacular instances of a general trend.[13]

However, after 1815 cattle and kelp prices began to fall dramatically, from £6 to £3 10s per beast and from £20 to £10 per ton for the latter. It was a sign of the growing tension that landlords who had been calling for a stop to emigration in the early 1800s (and who had successfully lobbied for the passing of the Passenger Vessels Act of 1803 which made emigration more difficult) were beginning to advocate wholesale clearance as the only solution by the 1820s. A dangerous, single-crop dependence had been created, as the partial potato failure of 1836 demonstrated. If the Highland landlords themselves had benefited, these policies might have been accounted a success, but already an increasing number of traditional chiefs were having to sell part or all of their estates to remain solvent. Some, like Sir Hector Mackenzie, 11th Laird of Gairloch, did try to lead from above by encouraging their crofters to improve their holdings and thus thin the population to a more stable structure which would allow movement in and out of the community as opportunity allowed, but they were lone voices, lacking the influence and support of their compeers. Gaelic Scotland thus retained its identity in this time of change, but as much because of its difficulties in controlling the pace of change as in its unique tradition of an ancient Celtic literature and language. The latter was generally discounted as a means of self-expression. Those who could afford it migrated to British North America. Those remaining were often confused: their loyalty seen as a sign of passivity; their lack of initiative, ironically, deplored by the very proprietors who refused to involve them in any decision-making about their economic future. Increasingly resentful and disenchanted, their only support by the 1830s came from Lowland voices who doubted the inevitable benefits of Whig economics and from the increasing numbers of their fellow gaels who had settled in lowland towns.

The new economic dynamism was most clearly evident in the industrial areas of the country, particularly in the new technologies being applied to the textile sector.[14] The basis for this had been laid in the previous half-century in the development of linen manufacture, output of which had jumped from about eight million yards in the 1750s to some twenty-four million yards by the 1800s. Exports of linen cloth counted for as much as 30 per cent of the value of total exports from Scotland by the 1790s. From this had sprung communities of full-time, skilled workers and employers. On to this structure, former linen masters like David Dale, James Finlay and James Monteith had grafted the even more flourishing cotton spinning industry. Powered at first by water, this growing sector was quite widespread geographically at the start, symbolised in large works such as Catrine in Ayrshire, the great showpiece of New Lanark, Deanston in Perthshire and the Woodside mills in Aberdeen, with many smaller establishments, particularly in the west of the country. By 1800 there were about 40 cotton factories, and by 1810 about 120, concentrated now through the increasing use of steam power in Glasgow and Paisley. By then, it was the country's premier manufacturing sector, having advanced to that position at what appeared to contemporaries to be alarming speed (Sir John Sinclair noting with concern in his *Statistical Analysis of Scotland* of 1826 that an ever-increasing number of workers, some 189 000, or about 1 : 10 of the total population, were becoming dependent on its fluctuating market fortunes[15]). By 1820, the value of its total output (about £7 million) was greater than the total agricultural rental of the country (around £5–6 million). These great units, with their large groups of workers disciplined by the regulating power of the machinery, symbolised the new power in the economy. In the 1830s, the industry was at its peak, with 198 factories employing about 36 000 people inside their walls, along with another 45 000–50 000 handloom weavers outside.

Equally important was the growth it stimulated in other innovative sectors such as cloth-printing, dyeing, chemical manufacture and general skill in machinemaking. At first subsidiaries of the cotton industry, these became great industries in their own right and continued to expand after cotton had reached its peak. Starting with the production of bleaching powder, a firm like Tennants of St Rollox moved on to become one of the greatest chemical works in Europe; while similarly great centres of dyeing and cloth printing were developed in the. Glasgow and Vale of Leven area. Although the advances were most spectacular in cotton, other textile sectors such as wool and linen manufacture were also transformed by spinning and weaving machinery. The former came to be concentrated in the borders around Galashiels and in the north-east, particularly in Aberdeen, the latter in the central and eastern Lowlands. At first, because of the .fibrous nature of flax, linen was dry spun, much of it in water-powered mills in the Fife and Angus countryside. However, a new method of wet-spinning was introduced in 1825, making it easier to use steam power. This led to a great spurt in the industry, causing towns like Dundee, Kirkcaldy and Arbroath to experience in the east coast the sort of growth – with all its associated strains – which had occurred earlier in the cotton towns of the west. By 1846 there were 36 flax-spinning factories in Dundee alone, compared with 17 in 1822.

In other areas of industry, such as iron and coal production, there was not the same spectacular advance. Nevertheless, the general population increase, along with the expansion in agriculture, in textiles and its associated industries, had stimulated growth in the number of ironworks and foundries and in the amount of coal being consumed. Much of the potential for further spectacular advance was, thus, already there in embryo before 1830. In 1828, J. B. Neilson had patented his discovery of the new 'hot blast' technology for smelting iron which, by dramatically cutting production costs, would lead soon to massive expansion in coal and iron production in the central belt. Even before this fundamental change in the size and character of the heavy industries had occurred, growing domestic and manufacturing demand had increased the number of iron foundries to more than 70 by 1825. Steamship and iron railroad systems were also being put in place. William Symington, who in conjunction with Patrick Miller and James Taylor had experimented with steam propulsion in 1788 on Dalswinton Loch, built a steamtug, the *Charlotte Dundas*, for the Forth and Clyde Canal in 1802, and by 1812 Henry Bell's steamship, the *Comet*, showed that sea-going steam travel was now a feasible proposition. In 1818, David Napier's *Rob Roy* was carrying passengers between the Clyde and Belfast. Glasgow's local statistician, James Cleland, noted that there were already 242 land steam engines and 68 marine steam engines in existence in the Clyde area by 1825. Coalfield development led to the creation of the Monkland to Kirkintilloch Railway Company, which started in 1826 and was being steam driven by 1831. A line linking the Dalkeith coalfields to Edinburgh was laid down between 1827 and 1831. By 1831 the Glasgow to Garnkirk line had been opened, steam driven and carrying passengers from the outset.

This world of embryonic industrialisation was being set in place by the desire to make use of the material world which the Enlightenment had encouraged among ordinary men of intelligence in Scotland. The background of its innovators was experimental and eclectic. The father of John Robertson, who built the steam engine for Henry Bell's *Comet*, had formerly been in charge of the cotton mill machinery at Catrine. J. B. Neilson was a colliery engineer, then a manager of a gasworks, with an interest in metallurgical chemistry which led him to the hot-blast process. David Mushet, who discovered the blackband ironstone layers in the central belt (the exploitation of which was made possible by the hot-blast process), was a metallurgist in Clyde Iron Works. Robert Addie, one of the early coal and iron developers in Lanarkshire, had been a small tenant farmer. David Elder, who became the manager of Robert Napier's Camlachie Foundry in 1821 and thus one of the founding figures of marine engineering on the Clyde, came from a family of traditional millwrights from the east of Scotland. Modernisation thus seemed to cast before it the outline of what the country was going to become.

It is clear, therefore, that in the pace of urbanisation, of work specialisation and the possibilities opened up by steam, many contemporaries saw a new age dawning. Statistics of population and town growth, as well as the state of urban society, struck them as apocalyptic. Much of it was still localised, however, and evident mainly in the west. Sir Archibald Alison was a prominent Tory lawyer, closely connected through his family with Edinburgh's cultural life. His description of the contrasts that he found when he arrived in Glasgow from Edinburgh, on becoming Sheriff of Lanarkshire in 1832, reads as if he had moved to a new country instead of simply some forty miles.[16] For the majority of the Scottish population up to about 1830, everyday life seemed to continue on the surface much as it had always done. The largest employers of labour were still in sectors such as agriculture, fishing and service trades. The inner-city areas of Glasgow and Edinburgh might have struck early nineteenth-century travellers as places of fearful squalor, and the industrial new towns as hell-holes of soot, flames and weekend bedlams. But these were in many ways still atypical. In the early 1830s many of the old landmarks still dominated the surface of Scottish life. The Established Church was still intact, and confident in its ability to renew itself. In both urban and rural Scotland, the old controllers with the old values and outlooks in administering the system still held sway. Much of the local government system and its educational and social welfare provision continued to be run by local elites. Landed groups still controlled large swathes of the country. Only in 1833, through the Burgh Reform Acts passed that year, did local government begin to change. Rural parishes only began to be brought under some degree of popular control and given some new powers with the Poor Law Amendment Act of 1845.

It could be said, therefore, that right up to the early 1830s, two Scotlands existed side by side, one modern, adventurous, tearing up the old and replacing it with the new, the other slower, still living in the afterglow of an older culture which still felt a sense of history, able to dismiss the problems of the new Scotland as the exception, and content to continue with administrative solutions built on traditional lines. No wonder, then, that responses to the challenges of this new age should often appear to be inconsistent and increasingly shrill. What might seem glaringly obvious for one area (such as general legislation to provide clean water supplies or ensure a minimum standard for the poor), might appear to entail a heavy burden of unnecessary new taxation for another. The strong regional variations in timing and experience meant that no overall approach easily suggested itself. This explains the continued acceptance of practices in the 1810s and 1820s which, only in hindsight, seem more suited to the eighteenth than to the nineteenth centuries in their insistence on parochial structures and community values of self-reliance and mutual support.

Nevertheless, even if there was no sudden overall change in Scottish economic and social life, it is clear that by the 1830s there was an open-endedness about developments and a continuous dynamism, an expectation of the new which made the older world seem increasingly remote. Costumes of knee breeches and powdered wigs could still fit into the world of 1800 or 1810. As time went on, they became increasingly anomalous in an 1830s world of longcoats, gartered long trousers and top hats. It was a society which gave new groups opportunities to emerge. It is sometimes assumed that the 'middle classes' in the nineteenth century were simply a continuation of an existing group, when the truth is that they had often risen recently from the lower ranks of the less undifferentiated society of the eighteenth century. David Dale had started by herding cattle in Stewarton in Ayrshire. The Monteiths had begun as working weavers: so had William Collins, before becoming a clerk in John Monteith's cotton mill about 1806, then a very successful private schoolmaster in 1813, and finally the founder of a famous publishing house in 1819. Elizabeth Grant of Rothiemurchus hints at this when she remarked of her visit to Glasgow in 1819 that it had become 'a mere manufacturing seaside town .... its merchants no longer the cadets of the neighbouring old County families, but their clerks of low degree shot up into the high places'. Her perspective, however, was from the wrong end – one which looked backwards to a more aristo-cratic age. Sir Archibald Alison was more perceptive in noting the new groupings adjusting uneasily to each other by the 1830s: 'The West In-dia merchants (the "Sugar Aristocracy") took the lead. . . . Next to these came the Cotton magnates . . . some of them possessed of great wealth and superior abilities . . . The Calico printers stood third, and last of all came the iron and coal masters many of them possessing greater wealth than all the others. . . . But there was no getting them to draw with each other'.[17] Thus there emerged new groups in the towns, uneasy with the status quo and increasingly ready to take a critical view, unsoftened by past association with the traditional institutions and elites.

Such social and economic developments were bound to affect intel-lectual and political boundaries. Some sought to find where they were going by looking anew at their past. The vogue for Romanticism started by Walter Scott in 1814 should not obscure the fact that much of the message in his Scottish historical novels such as *Waverley*, *Old Mortality* and *The Heart of Midlothian* was a hard-headed restatement of the con-servative rationalism of the Scottish Enlightenment. Extremes such as Jacobite and Whig, Presbyterian and Episcopalian, Unionist or anti-Unionist, Improver or Traditionalist, had to be reconciled by working together, sobered by experience, towards a better future which would not basically upset the existing social and political structure. It was a note that had already been sounded by the *Caledonian Mercury* at the end of the previous century when it declared: 'it is to trade, industry and the soil that we must look for improvement and not to the clamour and heat of politics'. Such 'clamour and heat', however, kept rearing its in-convenient head. The conflicting currents of Evangelicalism, Romantic-ism and Rational Enlightenment sharpened contemporary argument as to the direction to be taken and the values which should predomin-ate. It was obvious by the 1800s that Scottish society had experienced a remarkable degree of material progress without a corresponding growth in public participation in the direction of affairs. Appeals to the past by men rethinking their present situation were, thus, bound to cause argument as to which past should be recalled. At the opposite pole to Scott stood the Anti-Burgher minister, Thomas McCrie, whose biographies of *John Knox* (1811) and *Andrew Melville* (1819) were more than antiquarian examinations of the roots of Presbyterianism. McCrie's view of history did include the idea that the state should have the sanction of the popular will, and that religion and morality should influence the nation's mind and order its actions.[18]

The economic dynamism of the period meant that all groups were having to adjust their relationships to the means of production. The need to find an answer to the Adam Smith conundrum of how to achieve specialisation while avoiding alienation was becoming more pressing. The opportunities opened up by the new technology gave new freedom of action and decision-making to successful entrepreneurs and businessmen, but many others went bankrupt in the attempt. There were more rewards for the skilled workmen but wages and conditions could only be maintained by strict control over entry and apprenticeship. This became more difficult, however, as employers were able to draw on a widening labour pool, backed up by local justices and judges increasingly willing to circumvent the customary regulations protecting the trades. Responses ranged widely. At one extreme, the new market philosophy advised working folk to moderate their demands and earn prosperity and the respect of society via struggle and sacrifice. At the other, those looking back to the days of an older communal society argued that progress was part of a bargain in which those who had given up their rights to the land should still have a guaranteed place in an interdependent community. Some towns seemed to suffer less from these incipient class conflicts than others. Aberdeen, for all its growth, retained much of its old social homogeneity. So, to a lesser extent, did Edinburgh, because of the traditional interdependence between its governing classes and the tradesmen who serviced their needs. Inevitably, the new sense of social division was greatest in the western manufacturing districts.[19]

The democrats, strong among traditional trades like the handloom weavers who had imbibed the doctrines of Tom Paine, wanted a greater say for the people. Their cause had been in eclipse since the 1790s, when the atheistical and terrorist forces of the French Revolution took control and caused a general revulsion among ordinary people in Scotland. However, rejection of French excesses did not mean that all desire for rational change had been blotted out. It had simply receded into the background, ready to be brought forth when circumstances warranted it. County and, in particular, burgh reform movements which had flourished in the 1780s were beginning to revive once again in the 1810s. The Whigs, of course, had long felt that the paths to representation and power were laughably feudal and restrictive in Scotland. The founding of journals such as the *Edinburgh Review* in 1802 and newspapers like *The Scotsman* in 1817 marked their growing confidence. More significantly, the increasing numbers of regional newspapers critically discussing principles of policy and consent thereto – such as the *Dundee Advertiser*, which started in 1801 and drew much of its material from Cobbett – demonstrated a growing market for such concerns at a more general level lower down the social scale among the new urban artisans. The new business classes, with their belief in personal liberty and economic freedom, were also being forced into political considerations as they began to ponder by the 1800s how such freedoms were to be defended from taxes arbitrarily imposed by a system which obviously favoured some interests, and particularly the landed one, at the expense of others.[20]

Questions of how to make participation catch up with progress were kept to the fore by the resumption of war with Napoleon in 1803. His blockade and the British riposte of Orders-in-Council, which had the effect of hampering trade with the continent in 1806–8, began to turn the manufacturing classes against the government. Stories of peculation in high places, as at Henry Dundas' impeachment in 1805, scandals in the Vanity Fair atmosphere of the Regency, such as the Duke of York's mistress selling army commissions in 1809 in return for cash, heightened the feelings of alienation. Further down the social scale, the prosperity enjoyed by groups like the handloom weavers began to waver and finally crash. In 1812 their appeals to the justices to set an arbitrated wage level, which the judiciary itself had recommended as the alternative to striking, were flouted by their employers. A strike ensued which involved about 40 000 weavers and stretched as far as Aberdeen, but they found themselves outmanoeuvred and their leaders were imprisoned for restraint of trade. As judges and government thus came down increasingly on the side of market economics and away from guarantees of fair prices, opinion at all levels began to turn to the view that the remedy lay in political reform. The Corn Law of 1815, which prevented the importation of grain until home-grown supplies exceeded 80 shillings per quarter, demonstrated the way in which the restricted electoral system benefited the landed interest in Parliament, and provided middle- and working-class radicals with an issue that cut across class interests. The large popular protests and petitions from town councils which followed showed how widespread such convictions had become.[21]

The unemployment and distresses caused on the return to peace after 1815, as ex-soldiers and sailors tried to get back into the labour market at a time when both market demand and prices were falling, inevitably saw a sharp increase in the political temperature and the beginnings of a mass movement calling for reform. Following the visit by Major Cartwright to Scotland in 1815, a rash of reform clubs (advocating organised petitioning for measures such as universal manhood suffrage, annual parliaments and the ballot) had been formed. Such activity did not appear out of nothing. Rather, it was built on the efforts of those who had kept the cause of reform alive when it was dangerous to do so. In 1816, when the local authorities refused to provide facilities, some 40 000 turned up to support a reform meeting at Thrushgrove, on lands just on the northern edge of Glasgow, owned by a small shopkeeper and long-time radical, James Turner. Among others from this old reform group was Robert Grahame, a lawyer who had helped to defend the radicals of 1793 and who went on to become the first Reform Lord Provost of Glasgow. His brother had been a partner of Archibald Prentice, who later helped to start the Anti-Corn Law League in Manchester, who, in turn, was a cousin of David Prentice, editor of the radical *Glasgow Chronicle*. Archibald Prentice also had connections with the burgh reform group led by Archibald Fletcher. In Edinburgh it took some moral courage for a bookseller like Adam Black to stand up in the inauspicious surroundings of the Merchant Company in 1817 to speak in favour of burgh reform (and for his pains be told by an old Tory behind him, who tried to pull him down to prevent him speaking, 'Sit down man! Ye're ower young to speak' – Black was 33 years old at the time!). Such activity showed that men in the general run of society were beginning to act for themselves, a fact expressed in Sandy Rodger's mock ironical verses on the authorities' reaction to the Thrusgrove meeting:

> 'Vile "sooty rabble", what d'ye mean
> By raising a' this dreadfu' din,
> Do ye no ken what horrid sin
>         Ye are committing
> By haudin' up your chafts sae thin       [cheeks]
>         For sic a meeting? ...
> ... Base Rads! whose ignorance surpasses
> The dull stupidity of asses,
> Think ye the privileged classes
>         Care aught about ye?
> If ony mair ye daur to fash us,
>         By George! we'll shoot ye! ...'.[22]

Matters became more serious with the deepening economic distress from 1818, and some of the more radical elements began to speak of gaining their rights by direct action. News of Peterloo in August 1819 sparked off a number of large demonstrations in the western textile districts, with rioting in Paisley. April of 1820 saw placards appear calling for a general strike and rising. There were widespread stoppages lasting for a week, and some armed activity took place in Strathaven and in Glasgow, where a group of weavers marched out towards Falkirk hoping to meet up with like groups from England. These were routed by a detachment of hussars at Bonnymuir, with four being wounded and 19 captured. This 'Radical War' should not be dismissed because of the small numbers involved. The authorities were alarmed enough to try 47 people for treason (many others having fled before capture). Three were singled out as an example to be publicly executed by hanging and decapitation: Andrew Hardie, John Baird and James Wilson – all weavers. Twenty-one others were also found guilty but had their sentences commuted, most of them being transported.

The sentences were particularly savage, especially given the mitigation that might have been offered as to the amount of distress being suffered by the weavers and similar workers at this period. Nor did government try to play down the incident. That was left to moderate whigs such as Henry Cockburn who sought to distance 'respectable' reform from the spectre of social upheaval on continental lines by putting most of the blame on 'government exaggeration and public craze'. Such a theory hardly explains why the great mass of weavers took part for the best part of a week in what was, in effect, a general strike, or why those at Bonnymuir stood and fought the soldiers before surrendering; nor why there were associated violent demonstrations in places such as Paisley, Kilsyth, Balfron and Greenock. Its longer-term importance was that it paved the way for great reform meetings, like that at the Edinburgh Pantheon, held later in the same year, the first such demonstration that had been dared in the capital ever since the early 1790s. Compared to what had been threatened in April, gatherings of respectably dressed reformers calling for the King to dismiss his ministers seemed a tamer and safer way of venting public concern in the autumn of 1820 – especially when the prevailing theme appeared to be that reform must be attempted in order to avoid revolution.[23]

By the 1820s, therefore, in the field of public affairs, Scottish society had moved well beyond the point at which it had been in 1800 when the

Tories had been supreme. Now the position was reversed and the old governors were increasingly on the defensive. Changes in the public mood played a significant part in these developments. The eighteenth century had seen a widespread belief take root, quite far down in Scottish society, that progress and improvement would inevitably come from an understanding of the laws of nature and social organisation. The mechanistic tendency in this outlook had been given a severe jolt by the American and French Revolutions, and by the social and economic upheavals of the early nineteenth century. As a result, a more sombre mood emerged, bringing with it a deeper sense of the individual's responsibility for the state of society: progress was to be personal, associated with moral worth and not merely mental. In this way the Enlightenment continued to be a prime force among all classes in Scottish society, but now it was increasingly allied with a growing feeling that the tone of public life should be raised.

This new attitude found its readiest expression in a revived sense of evangelicalism, which was part of a general post-1815 trend affecting all churches throughout Europe. In the Church of Scotland this showed itself in the growing strength of the Evangelical group, who now challenged the traditionally dominant Moderates with increasing confidence; as, for instance, in 1805 when they prevented the latter's nominee gaining the chair of mathematics at Edinburgh University. Their attempts to revive the Established Church's sense of mission and oppose unfettered lay patronage put them at odds with those who wished to continue the old methods of government by an inner circle, but found an increasingly influential voice in *The Edinburgh Christian Instructor*, established in 1810. There had been a marked growth of Baptists and Congregationalists since the 1790s, while the two main bodies of dissent in Scotland, the Seceders and the Relief Church, both of which had broken away from the Church of Scotland in the previous century, had always been evangelical in outlook. Since these drew their members largely from the classes profiting from the social and economic expansion of these years, they were now becoming ever more numerous and influential. The majority of the Seceders had also come to the view, on grounds of religious liberty, that conscience and not the state should be the guarantor of belief, and in 1820 had formed themselves into the United Secession. This 'voluntary' principle had always been held by the Relief church, so that its spread led to increasing questioning of the statutory position of the Church of Scotland and its ministers. This inevitably placed them at odds with the traditional governing groups intent on maintaining the institutions of the country as they always had been.[24]

The decade also continued to see growing evidence of the need for burgh reform. Self-electing oligarchies narrowly drawn from the merchant guildry and trade incorporations ran the royal burghs. This had been a recipe for maladministration and venality for years. Not all towns were badly run: Glasgow and Irvine are examples of large and medium-size towns which were managed well on the whole, despite the system. In many others, however, the reverse was true. Some large towns, such as Edinburgh, Aberdeen and Dundee, had become insolvent. In others, public property had been alienated to the advantage of the councillors, and their friends and relatives had been too often favoured with public custom or official posts. The ready welcome given to John Galt's novel *The Provost* (1822), with its ironic and realistic portrayal of burgh life as manipulated by Provost Pawkie to his and his cronies' self-perpetuating interest, showed how near the mark it was. An increasing number of towns were adopting local Police Acts, bypassing the existing town councils, to give the ratepayers greater say in how their money should be spent. Even the Tory administration recognized that the time for change had come when it proposed, just before it fell in 1830, a Burgh Police Act for Scotland which would include a system of popular election.

An underlying concern with the nature of power and how it should be exercised can also be discerned at another level, in the apparently random eruptions of localised industrial conflict in this decade which often contain within them common themes giving them wider continuity and coherence. Combinations of cotton spinners in the west of Scotland and of flax hecklers in the east, for instance, in their disputes in the 1820s over day-to-day industrial conditions, were also challenging their masters' claim to manage without any workers' participation. The cotton spinners put it succinctly in 1824: '. . . by the caprices of fortune there are many masters and managers who would have fitted a more dependent situation while the operatives of this country possess an information and general behaviour which entitle them to rather more respect than the proud and wealthy are willing to accord them . . .'. Such mingling of social and economic relationships with political overtones of a more general nature had become a common item in the pages of the widely selling working men's *Herald to the Trades Advocate* during its brief existence in 1830–31.[25]

Nevertheless, these new outlooks did not lead immediately to change. In part, this was due to the more circumspect way in which the liberal Tories governed after 1822 under Liverpool and Canning. But it was also because of the obvious fact that any change in Scotland would have to wait until the question of reform in Britain as a whole had been settled. The inadequacies of the Scottish electoral system were glaringly obvious. Its share of representation at Westminster had been frozen at the Union in 1707 at 45 MPs in the Commons (30 for the counties and 15 for the royal burghs) and 16 Representative Peers in the Lords, taking no account of the marked increase in population and wealth which had developed since then. The franchise, too, still remained in its feudal state. In the counties, the possession of land – no matter how extensive – did not confer the vote. Only the limited number of those holding property directly from the Crown at a certain valuation (£400 Scots), the county freeholders, could do so. Since these 'superiorities', not actual possession of property, conferred the vote, they could be broken up into parcels of sufficient valuation to 'make interest' and, indeed, they were openly advertised for sale in the press. The result was an artificially restricted electorate in the counties, numbering only 2889 in 1823, many of them nominal or fictitious. Winning or losing elections had come to depend on how many such votes each side could command.[26] Also, despite the growing importance of commercial Scotland, only the 66 royal burghs returned MPs, leaving large developing urban areas like Paisley, Airdrie and Greenock, unrepresented. Within this structure, Edinburgh alone returned its own MP. The others were grouped, large and small, into 14 constituencies each containing four or five burghs, whose town councillors (about 1400 overall) chose a delegate to vote for them at elections. Differing rates of development since 1707 had produced anomalies. Glasgow (population 202 400 in 1831) was many times larger than the other three towns combined in its group (10 300), but had no more say than them. Similarly, small east coast burghs such as Inverbervie or St Andrews had a voice just like Aberdeen or Dundee, which had long outgrown them. Since any efforts to make the town councils more representative would fundamentally alter the system, any hope of burgh reform had to be subordinated to parliamentary reform.[27]

When it did come, change emerged from national events which showed that the king's ministers could no longer ignore the changes going on in British society. Wellington, who succeeded Canning in 1828, was forced to concede Catholic Emancipation in 1829 by events in Ireland. This divided the Tories badly, its ultras especially feeling themselves betrayed, and in 1830 a Whig government headed by Earl

Grey, pledged to some kind of reform, took office. These events marked the beginning of modern political life in Scotland. The English Reform Act of 1832 laid down the basic principles that were incorporated into the subsequent Scottish Act. These were, first, to widen the electoral base and, second, to make the constituencies more representative of the changes which had occurred in the country's social and economic life. Property holders of £10 valuations, in both the counties and the burghs, plus substantial tenants in the former (mainly at £50 rentals), could now vote, which had the effect of ensuring that as property and population grew so too would the electorate. In England, this resulted in a significant widening of the electorate.[28] In Scotland, the effect could truthfully be described as revolutionary in creating a new electorate of 33 000 voters in the counties and 31 000 in the burghs (in stark contrast to the pre-1832 electorate of some 4500). Ayrshire, for example, which had contained only some 147 voters, a number of them nominal, now had over 3100 true voters after 1832. The number of constituencies had also been increased from 45 to 53, all of the new seats going to urban areas, with two each to Glasgow and Edinburgh, one each to Dundee, Aberdeen, Perth, Paisley and Greenock, and the other 14 to groups of burghs, which now included some of the new urban areas. This might seem minuscule in a total Parliament of 658 members but its psychological effect was enormous in a country in which institutional immobility had come to be regarded as a virtue.

Not surprisingly, at the time these reforms were painted as if they were the solution to all ills. They certainly went a long way in repairing the worst defects of the old system. How satisfactory they were for an evolving society was less certain. Confusion appeared at once as to the basis of the property qualifications on which voters claimed to be enrolled, leading to a series of anomalies. More seriously, the qualification level of £10 had been set at a level that seemed sensible in England. In Scotland, however, with its overall lower standard of living, this excluded many who would otherwise have been entitled to vote. Despite the apparently revolutionary jump in the numbers of voters, enfranchisement levels in Scotland remained seriously below those in the rest of the Britain for many years. Only 1 in 38 of the population were enfranchised in Scotland, compared to about 1 in 20 of the population in England – an imbalance which only began to lessen in the later nineteenth century. In addition, although all the new seats went to towns, the switch had hardly been fair. The Scottish Tories were among the most unyielding in their defence of the old system, and they mounted a highly successful rearguard action in keeping the Scottish county representatives at 30. This meant fewer representatives for the larger numbers crammed into the city constituencies. The Highland region, with a population of 389 000, retained eight seats (Argyll, Inverness, Ross and Cromarty, Sutherland, Caithness, Orkney and Shetland, Wick and Inverness Burghs), whereas Glasgow and Edinburgh, with a combined population of 362 000, received only four between them. The four largest towns (including Leith), containing a fifth of the country's population and nearly a third of the electorate, had only a ninth of the MPs (six out of 53). Since urban Scotland continued to grow at the expense of the rural areas during the century, this political weighting became ever more anomalous. In addition, grouping had been retained which allowed small and anachronistic burghs to hang on at the expense of more thriving places. Lastly, the question of how Scotland was to be represented was bound to remain open, since its growing importance in population and wealth was hardly reflected by an increase of only eight MPs.[29]

In the immediate term, however, this reformulation of the Scottish political nation meant that burgh reform need no longer be delayed. Thus, by two Burgh Reform Acts in 1833, the town councils in the royal burghs and the new parliamentary burghs were to be elected by the £10 property holders, and publish their accounts. More importantly, the needs of modern towns for efficient policing, regular paved streets, water supplies, adequate lighting, cleansing and drainage were dealt with by an accompanying 1833 Burgh Police Act, which gave the residents (again at the £10 level) in royal burghs and burghs of barony power to provide such services. Once again, however much these acts answered the problems of the past, their effectiveness in meeting future needs was less certain. As with the 1832 Parliamentary Act, the qualification level disbarred quite a few who had had a say in their burgh's administration before 1833, and prevented many more who were otherwise qualified from controlling their immediate governors. The Burgh Police Act was a step in the right direction, for the Scottish definition of 'police' provided more extensive powers, particularly in regard to public health, than were available in England. However, borrowing powers were limited; the police powers and duties that it provided were adoptive, not compulsory; and while the more enlightened localities began to move in the direction of the greater regulation and order thus provided, many more whose needs were just as pressing did not.[30]

Some adopted only the parts of the legislation that suited them, and the wider vision which had often accompanied arguments for civic improvement in the earlier parts of the century began to recede. Ratepayer considerations meant that money tended to be spent on the paving and policing of the better areas, while lighting the commercial centres to prevent nocturnal crime became a greater priority than planning for better communal water supplies. More seriously, the 1833 Burgh Police Act did not meet the needs of the suburbs or of the many new towns, such as Johnstone, Galston or Coatbridge, which were developing because of the quickening pace of industrial growth, since it applied only to the £10 inhabitants of existing royal burghs and burghs of barony.[31]

Thus, in the political as in the social and economic developments of this period, much of the old remained in place. It would be wrong to dismiss the Reform Acts of 1832 and 1833 as being of limited effect. The truth is that they changed the country's ways of making decisions about itself quite fundamentally. Before 1832, Scotland had been managed from above. After 1832, it could no longer be manipulated politically by a single faction, and it was hoped that it would manage itself from within in a more harmonious, rational fashion. But the question of how its institutions and legal system would function in an evolving, dynamic society was left in abeyance, in the expectation that these would somehow sort themselves out. The electoral system which replaced that of the pre-1832 era represented an enormous change. However, much of it remained potential, a spur to further activity rather than a present solution. The MPs elected after 1832 tended in social background and attitudes to be very much like those who had been returned before then. It took time for the new system to begin to meet the pressures facing Scottish society as a result of the fundamental shifts in its economic and social life, and for it to reflect adequately the sort of issues that concerned the new electorate. The most obvious immediate change came in the reformed burghs as new interest groups, particularly of radical seceders, began to be returned as town councillors.[32]

By the 1830s, therefore, while much had changed, much still remained the same on the surface. The majority of people still did not live in manufacturing areas, and while the older structures of church and local government – and the culture that underpinned them – might be ceasing to function effectively in the largest towns, they still managed to survive in the more localised environments in the rest of the country. However, a watershed had clearly been crossed by 1832 and the processes of development were becoming irresistible. The older rural society was itself becoming increasingly specialised and ordered. The pace was being set by the urban manufacturing areas. Demands for wider political participation continued to be sounded, particularly from those in the working classes who had been promised votes in return for support at the great political demonstrations of 1830 and 1831, only to find that £10 barriers had been erected against them. The values behind movements as diverse as anti-patronage or temperance or radical demands for 'free trade' were now forcing parties and institutions into new paths which would determine the political and cultural context of the future. Henry Cockburn, the prominent judge and leading Edinburgh Whig, remarked perceptively in 1845 that all the great issues of his day (Reform, Church, Free Trade) had had their rise in an older soil.[33] In the new political context created by the reforms of 1832, the Scots increasingly came to share a common interest with their fellow Britons in adjusting to the new challenges of this period. However, in each of these 'great internal questions' as to how the country should be governed, which values should prevail, how its population should earn its living, their perspectives and actions were bound to be conditioned by their own previous history and social ethos and by their own experience of the pace of modernisation. Its internal development within the greater British whole was to be increasingly scrutinised and reappraised. The transitions of this period presaged a century of continuing expansion and adaptation.

# 2

# A NEW SOCIETY: 1832–50

Scottish society continued to be profoundly affected by economic change in the 1830s and 1840s. Neilson's demonstration in 1828 that iron could be produced more cheaply by blowing hot air into the blast furnace gave the ironmasters the means to exploit the vast untapped coal and iron ore resources that existed in central Scotland. Hitherto, the iron industry had developed steadily, if not particularly spectacularly, in response to local demand, from 23 000 tons in 1800 to 37 500 tons in 1830 (5 per cent of total British output). The hot blast process, however, by cutting fuel production costs dramatically, now allowed the ironmasters to compete successfully in the British and overseas market just when world demand for iron was burgeoning. By 1840 they were producing 241 000 tons (25 per cent of British output), from a rapidly growing number of ironworks throughout the central belt, principally in Lanarkshire and Ayrshire. By 1851, output had soared to 775 000 tons.

Such phenomenal growth surpassed anything experienced during the earlier revolution in textile manufacture. Then there had been some attempt to plan for the new workforces. This new development required large amounts of labour immediately which could be hired and fired to meet fluctuations in market demand. The whole thing had something of a frontier-like atmosphere about it, dominated by a handful of rough-diamond ironmasters such as the Bairds or the Merrys, literally scooping up vast profits from the soil around them and dragging in their wake transient workforces housed in boom towns with few amenities. As one rather dazzled commentator put it, perhaps more aptly than he realized: 'Fortunes have been realised here in the iron trade with a rapidity only equalled by the sudden and princely gains of the adventurers who accompanied Pizarro to Peru'.[1] Output on such a scale could not be wholly absorbed within the country, and the greater part of it went to England or overseas, thus tying the fortunes of the country even more to international demand. By 1850, 90 per cent of British pig-iron exports came from Scotland. All of this forced the coal-mining sector into similar expansion, further underlining the economic importance of the west of the country. Coal output, which had been rising steadily, shot up from the mid-1830s. By 1841, there were 33 000 miners in Scotland compared with only some 8000 at the start of the century, most of them now in the fast-developing western coalfields. Since most of this labour was new, made up of those losing jobs elsewhere in Scotland or Ireland, ready to work for wages and conditions below those won by the old collier communities, it split up the homogeneity of the workforce and made it easier for the ironmasters to dominate the industry. The resulting divisions and vulnerability added to the pell-mell atmosphere of the times.[2]

The engineering sector, especially on its marine side, also grew in this period. Marine engineers, like David and Robert Napier, headed a remarkable group who linked the forges and foundries of the region with the needs of shippers for faster and larger freight carriers. Their ability to improve boilers, increase capacity by the use of iron for hulls and perfect screw propulsion attracted increasing custom in developing the Atlantic and other trade routes, and made the Clyde, although not yet the largest, one of the most technically advanced shipbuilding sites in Britain by the 1840s.[3] These were only the most spectacular in a whole range of other engineering trades growing in the region, not so much because of the cheapness and proximity of the raw materials – although that was undoubtedly a factor – as from local ability to meet specific customer demands for new products. What bound them all together was the creation at this time of a national railway network, with all its multiplier effects. Glasgow and Edinburgh were linked in 1842, then in 1846 Edinburgh was connected with England via Berwick, as was Glasgow, via Annandale, in 1848. By 1850, the area north of Perth was being developed up to Aberdeen.

In spite of the very real geographical problems of terrain in Scotland, the country was thus integrated in a way never before realised, with effects that were psychological as well as material. It speeded up the whole pace of life, giving greater stability and certainty to suppliers and customers. Wider markets could be tapped, the rapid access to England being particularly important. This had obvious advantages for the in-

dustrial areas in the west, but it also served to reinforce the strong regional activities already in place in the Borders or around Aberdeen
and Dundee and their hinterlands. While it was important that a
Glasgow merchant was now only nine hours away from the English
Midlands, it was just as significant for a cattle producer in the north-east
to be able to go to and from Aberdeen in a day. In addition to the new
employment it created to operate and service the network, it also
boosted the construction industry through the experience it provided
in handling vast quantities of materials and men.[4] A more mundane
example is the extra demand it generated for paper for posters, time-
tables, tickets, bills of lading and general stationery.

Despite these rapid advances in iron, coal and engineering, it would
be wrong to view the whole social experience of this time in the light of
their impact alone. The older textile sectors continued to be important,
with significant new developments in thread and carpet making, while
the steady expansion of regions such as the north-east provided a coun-
terpoint to what was going on in the west. The economic changes of this
period resemble not so much a series of spectacular volcanic upheavals
as so many currents swirling back and forth, building up layers of activity which, like geological formations, folded over and intermixed with
each other. The cotton industry might no longer be in the lead, but it
remained a very large employer of labour, and its offshoots such as
dyeing continued to be highly profitable and successful. The woollen
industry, too, remained buoyant in the Borders and the Stirling area. In
the east of Scotland, the rapid development of the jute industry in
Dundee from the 1840s onwards reinforced the significance of the
coarse textile trade there. Dundee was also notable as a shipbuilding
centre, as was Aberdeen, whose long-distance sailing ships, the 'clip-
pers', were internationally famous by mid-century. Aberdeen's varied
economy also included granite, paper making, textiles and its cattle
trade, the latter being particularly boosted by the arrival of the railway.
Such growth, although less dramatic than in the west, led to great expansion in the harbour and dock facilities all the way down the east
coast from Aberdeen to the Forth, with consequent demand for such
essential equipment as cranes, rail and shed machinery.[5]

Since this second great phase of growth and expansion was more
widespread, and since it took place during years which saw severe economic downturns in the later 1830s and the early and later 1840s, it
created great strains as society tried to cope. There was a sense of crisis
accompanying the changes of this period different from that experi-

enced in the earlier part of the century. There was a more general realisation that, despite the heady evidence of growth, conditions were somehow beginning to worsen. The movement of prices and wages up to mid-century suggest that while skilled workers might make marginal gains in this growing economy, the many more unskilled whom it had called forth did not. For each cotton spinner making top wages, for instance, there were another seven mill workers, mainly female, who were paid very much less; in traditional sectors such as the building trades or metal working, each craftsman depended on a number of labourers. What the skilled gained in periods of advance could just as quickly be lost during subsequent downturns, the unskilled finding it even harder to regain lost ground. The largest manufacturing group at this time, the handloom weavers, were being remorselessly squeezed into starvation as more and more flocked into the trade and the number of factory steamlooms grew. From 58 000 in 1800, their numbers had peaked at around 80 000 in 1840, and their rapid decline to only 25 000 by 1850 indicates terrible social trauma.[6] The same decade also saw the Highland crofting community experiencing its worst ever subsistence crisis.

General environmental conditions also appeared to worsen in these years, with widespread outbreaks of fever in 1818, 1826, 1837, 1843 and 1847, interspersed with visitations of cholera in 1832 and 1848–9. Familiarity with death and sickness made people feel more vulnerable. Local estimates of death rates in the urban areas at this time could be as high as 30 per 1000, soaring to over 40 per 1000 during epidemics. After 1855, when official statistics began to be collected, national death rates averaged between 21 and 24 per 1000 until 1880 when they finally began to fall, concealing much higher rates in the inner-city areas; and since some institutional and legal responses were beginning to remedy the situation by mid-century, conditions must have been worse during these earlier years of greater strain and less preparedness. Contemporaries were also beginning to note how the towns were becoming more congested, increasing numbers being accommodated either by subdividing existing houses or in industrial blocks with few amenities. The worst examples of these were the rows of 'single-ends' in the iron and coal towns, overshadowed by the open-topped furnaces, some divided by pit entries, and all of them lacking indoor water.

Housing standards had always been low in Scotland, not only in the Highlands but even in the advanced agricultural areas where progress was slow and uneven. In 1842, houses in an ancient burgh like Tain were still usually one- or two-roomed, earthen-floored and damp, sur-rounded by pigsties and family filth. At the other end of the country, Luss village was described in 1838 as a squalid place.[7] Since the new-comers to the industrial areas came from such backgrounds, it is not surprising that they accepted the makeshifts provided. Even so, they had never lived so packed together in the countryside, and when of-ficial figures on housing were eventually provided by the 1861 Census of Scotland, the results shocked social reformers. These showed that 34 per cent of all families in Scotland lived in one room and another 37 per cent in two rooms. Edinburgh (with 64 per cent of its families in one and two rooms) only seemed better when compared with Glasgow (73.4 per cent), Aberdeen (74 per cent), Dundee (79.6 per cent) and Paisley (80.8 per cent). Not surprisingly, social investigators found much evidence of squalor and wretchedness, particularly in the great towns, during these decades; and for the majority of families, particularly women, life was a constant battle against dirt and disease. In addition, since these were the years during which increasing numbers were being drawn into the dangerous environments of cotton and jute factories, of coal mines and iron works there was more likelihood of breadwinners suffering indus-trial injury or sickness causing more families to fall into the lower ranks as earnings were reduced or tools pawned.

However, to picture society in these years solely in such negative terms would be too crude. The ability of people to survive and set down some roots constantly modifies the black and white view portrayed by the Blue Books of the period. Despite the long hours and debilitating conditions, there is constant evidence in the press of a lively popular culture. Country tradesmen, for instance, continued to enjoy curling competitions and quoiting in the 1830s and 1840s. Also, it must have taken time and a great deal of organisational skill to prepare the bands and banners which were always prominent features at the political and trade demonstrations of this period. When Daniel O'Connell visited Scotland in 1835, his triumphal progress from Edinburgh to Glasgow was marked by well-organised processions of welcome from the Trades. Temperance societies were organising day trips for their mem-bers to the Clyde coast in the 1840s.[8]

The truth is that there was a remarkable growth in voluntary self-help activities aimed at improving people's educational skills and develop-ing their self-reliance in this period. Much of this, of course, was encour-aged from above as a way of inculcating the lessons of *laissez-faire* economics, particularly the futility of strikes. But it was more than a crude form of social control. Many working men who advocated the virtues of thrift and temperance, and of the need for working men to be informed, were the very ones who argued in pamphlets, newspapers and Chartist groups that economic development should be controlled as well as welcomed. Membership of a Temperance society with its encouragement of thrift could also be an assertion of working men's independence, as well as a much needed safeguard against the degradation of their surroundings. The formal and informal institutions of the state were too limited in their ability to defend them against long hours and fragmentary education, so they had to build their own protective alternatives through organisation. There was thus some common ground between philanthropists and workingmen in reforming ventures of this sort. Both were critical of the workings of present society and both believed that a better society would result from individual improvement. Often, these ventures started off by being led from above and were then taken over by the groups they were intended to lead. This was the case with the Temperance movement, started in 1829 by the Greenock lawyer John Dunlop and soon joined by William Collins. Branches spread rapidly throughout the country, and by 1844 these were united in a Scottish Temperance League. A movement such as this, opposed to the prevailing customs, given to social criticism and independent expression, appealed to radicals. It is no surprise that John Fraser, editor of the Chartist newspaper, *The True Scotsman*, helped found the temperance movement in Edinburgh; nor that John Murdoch, later leader of the highland crofters, was its life-long advocate as a means of making men free to defend themselves. It found an echo in the principles of Co-operation, which also began to grow markedly in this period, encouraged by pioneers such as Alexander Campbell who had been involved in the earlier Orbiston communitarian experiment. Campbell's idea of dividing profits among members according to the amount purchased epitomised the alliance of thrift, self-education and community improvement.[9]

Official Scotland's definition of and response to the problems of the time was often as piecemeal as the forces causing them. Local government was just beginning to develop in its modern form after 1833, and the idea of permanent and experienced administrative units found little general acceptance until the later 1840s. Public health suffered because outbreaks of fever or cholera tended to be met by temporary responses which were wound up as soon as the emergency passed. By 1850, only a minority of burghs (41) had adopted police powers under the 1833

Act. Municipalities such as Glasgow, Edinburgh, Aberdeen, Dundee and Paisley preferred to use local acts, but some large royal burghs, like Stirling, appear not to have adopted any powers. What is remarkable about many of those who did adopt the 1833 Act is how narrow the tax base was on which they had to build local services. Old Aberdeen, a burgh of barony, which was reputed to regulate its lamplighting according to the brightness of the moon, may have been an extreme case, but it was symptomatic of a more general trend. Only with the new and more extensive 1850 Police Act, which now enabled any 'populous place' (whether or not they were burghs) with a population of at least 1200 to become a police burgh, did such deficiencies begin to be repaired.[10]

The Established Church was also under pressure to change, partly to reinforce its authority in the new society that was emerging and partly to respond to the increasing signs of alienation and decline in community morale. With so much of the country's parochial administration in areas such as education and poor relief run by the Church, it could hardly remain immune. Unfortunately, its efforts to achieve the first of these aims increasingly diverted attention away from the second. Men like Thomas Chalmers, the famous evangelical and social theorist, wanted to defend the Church from its critics by making it a more effective and popular body, building more churches with government help in the growing industrial areas and modifying patrons' choice of ministers so as to make them more acceptable to the local community. When the Evangelicals gained a majority in the General Assembly in 1834, they set about implementing their programme by two measures. By the Veto Act, no presentee was to be intruded on a congregation against the wishes of its members. If a majority of heads of families objected to a patron's nominee, the Presbytery was bound to reject him. By the Chapel Act, chapels set up in populous areas were to be admitted to full parity as ecclesiastical parishes in the church courts. Since these were always the result of religious enthusiasm, their presence added to the Evangelical strength in the Established Church. Such moves immediately brought the Church into collision with the United Secession and the Relief Church who objected to revived competition just at a time when they themselves were expanding so successfully. In addition, fear of what might result from Roman Catholic Emancipation in 1829 had now transformed their voluntaryism from a principle by which they ordered their own affairs into a crusade against the whole idea of a national religion established by law.

Such a situation was fraught with difficulties, although many of them were as yet unseen in 1834. The weakness in the Veto Act was that it ignored the acknowledged authority of the presbytery to judge on matters of ecclesiastical fitness. The problem in the Chapel Act was that creating parishes was a civil as well as a religious responsibility, so that it raised the whole difficult issue of the respective boundaries of the jurisdiction claimed by Church and State. In addition, men such as Chalmers had reluctantly accepted the Veto as a way of avoiding the growing demand for the outright abolition of patronage, but once stuck with the policy they found it increasingly difficult to draw back. They also believed – perhaps naively, since they did not have it in writing – that the new Whig government had promised its support for their stance. Although there was a clear majority in the Assembly for these measures, a substantial and well organised minority of Moderates opposed them; thus, those setting the Church on its new course were beset by enemies within as well as without.

A series of court cases began to widen the whole issue from a struggle between Evangelical and Moderate, and Church and Dissent, to the more dangerous ground of Church–State relations. In 1838 the Court of Session decided that the Veto Act was *ultra vires* and, on appeal to the House of Lords, this was confirmed in terms that severely circumscribed the ecclesiastical jurisdiction claimed by the Vetoists (or Non-Intrusionists as they now began to be called). Beset by the taunts of the Voluntaries, who saw all this as proof of the ineffectiveness of religious establishments, they decided to press ahead with the principle of Non-Intrusion while seeking aid from the government in the shape of some form of amending legislation.[11] While these moves were taking place, a presbytery in Aberdeenshire, Strathbogie, became the focus of attention when a majority of its members decided to follow the civil courts rather than the Veto, and were first suspended in 1840, and then deposed in 1841 for their pains. Up to the later 1830s, the Conservatives had been sympathetic to the Church, but now Peel refused to act until the Strathbogie ministers were reinstated. By then all attempts at compromise were doomed. Finally, in 1842 the Chapel Act was also declared invalid by the civil courts, and this had the effect of calling all the actions taken by the Church while chapel ministers had sat in its courts into question. The Non-Intrusionists submitted a *Claim of Right* to the Conservative government, detailing their grievances and asserting their liberties as traced in Scottish history, only to have it rejected. In May 1843, to the surprise of the politicians who had badly misjudged the situation ever since the outset, an enormous secession took place of about a third of the parish ministers and their congregations. This was sufficient to justify the claim of this new Free Church of Scotland that it represented a Disruption of the true church from the state to which it would return once its claims of sovereignty in its own sphere had been acknowledged. Some areas were greatly affected by this exodus, particularly the major cities and the northern and western Highlands. In Aberdeen, all of the city ministers left their charges; and in Glasgow seven out of the ten churches in the Royalty[12] became vacant and three-quarters of the university's theology students joined the Free Church, as did all of the staff at David Stow's Normal School. In Edinburgh presbytery, about 60 per cent seceded. In most of Argyll, Inverness, Wester Ross and Sutherland, the parish churches were deserted. Almost at once, about 700 Free Church congregations came into existence.[13]

The Disruption was a significant turning-point in nineteenth-century Scotland. In many ways it marked the beginnings of its modern era. It broke whatever cultural coherence the old Kirk had retained in claiming to speak for the nation. Thereafter, its institutional role as a primary agent of local government became increasingly difficult to sustain. The emergence of this great new body added tremendous weight and status to Dissent in Scotland. It provided Highland crofters with a focus around which they could unite. It confirmed the new middle classes, who formed its backbone, in their view that the aristocratic forces which governed the country could no longer be trusted. Although the Whigs had been equally unhelpful, it was the Conservatives' misfortune to be in office after 1841 when the crisis came, so that all the opprobrium and bitter resentment felt by the Free Church was directed at them. From now on, its members became intent on turning the Liberals into a more radical weapon with which to beat the Conservatives.[14] All of this went a large way to make the former the dominant – indeed, the only real – political force in Scotland up to 1886. More indirectly, it reflected the growing pluralism of Scottish society and its free-trade philosophy, by forcing the various denominations after 1843 to compete for support as measured in the commitment of their membership.

It was also significant occurring when it did – during the unrest of the Chartist and Anti-Corn Law agitations, and just as the potato famine struck first Ireland in 1845 and then the Scottish Highlands in 1846, causing further great migrations to the central belt. Although many more Irish immigrants came to England, where they constituted 2.9

per cent of the population in 1851, their impact was greater in Scotland, where the 207 367 Irish-born in 1851 represented some 7.2 per cent of a smaller, more self-contained society. Altogether, allowing for deaths and further migration to America, about 110 000 Irish settled in Scotland during the 1840s. The Irish already here had been hopefully searching for work and a better life. Those coming after 1846 were fleeing famine and fever. Their numbers, already high in the western areas, shot up still further and spread out through the coalfields on to the eastern areas of the country, such as Edinburgh or Stirlingshire.[15] In towns like Dundee, they made up 18 per cent of the population, as well as a large number of its jute workers, by mid-century. Their appearance in the streets of the towns, often in rags and already ill with fever, intensified the strains of the 1840s. Desperate for work, their presence, like that of any large alien group, aroused resentment. In the aftermath of the Disruption, with its associated anxiety for the country's reformed tradition, so too did their culture and religion. The mood of many was expressed in the comments of the Registrar-General, made as late as 1871: '[the] invasion of the Irish race which attained enormous dimensions after 1840 . . . is likely to produce far more serious effects on the population of Scotland than even the invasion of the warlike hordes of Saxons, Danes, Norsemen . . . such a body of labourers of the lowest class, with scarcely any education, cannot but have most prejudicial effects on the population. As yet the great body of the Irish do not seem to have improved by their residence among us . . .'. Other more objective evidence would suggest that they were a more varied, resilient community than the undifferentiated mass he suggested. They showed considerable powers of adaptation in getting jobs and building up a framework of schools and parishes, just as the Presbyterians had been trying to do, as a means of stabilising themselves in a strange industrial environment. Only the need to earn a living from an early age prevented them from taking greater advantage of the schools that they helped to fund. Among the groups settled before the Famine influx there had also grown up a fairly strong degree of political independence and self-help ventures, and it is significant that, despite the rootlessness and disorientation caused by the traumas of the mid-1840s, they were sufficiently well organised to be able to question candidates at the 1852 general election.[16]

The failure of the potato crop in 1846 also caused great misery in the Highlands which lasted to the middle of the 1850s. By 1847, reports were coming in of thousands starving in the western coastal areas, and it was estimated that about two-thirds of the food supply of the labouring population had been lost. What prevented a calamity of Irish proportions was swift action by Relief Committees in the Lowlands, such as that organised by the Free Church, support by landlords for their tenants, and the coordination of these efforts by the Government's agents like Sir Charles Trevelyan, with the allocation of public money (through the Drainage Act) for estate improvement. The demand for labour in railway building in 1846 and 1847, together with traditional alternatives such as temporary migration and fishing, also helped, although too many crofters had to sell their cattle stocks in order to survive. Prevailing opinion blamed the crofters for their dependence on the potato, but social reformers like W. P. Alison struck nearer home in declaring that it was 'the absence of skill and capital to give them work rather than the presence of the potato to keep them alive which ought to fix the attention of those who wish to see the resources of the country developed'.[17] Given the sketchy system of poor relief in the Highlands (this was a chore left to estate factors rather than the church) the pressure of numbers on local resources could hardly be blamed on a too generous public welfare system. Trevelyan's views, however – that self-reliance had to be encouraged at all costs – prevailed, and by 1850 the emphasis had changed from immediate relief to emigration as the long-term solution. Some of this was encouraged by government-subsidised schemes such as that to Australia; but much was effected by eviction, coercion and forced emigration from estates, particularly in the outer and inner Hebrides and western mainland areas like Knoydart. Relief was only given in return for labour and only after stringent 'destitution tests'. The numbers thus forced out were very great, with some parishes losing up to half of their population in this period; and the rapidity of these removals, outstripping that of earlier clearances, made them all the more traumatic.[18] The numbers on the Macdonnel estate in Knoydart fell from 600 to 70 between 1847 and 1853, from 500 to 150 in the Ulva estate in Mull between 1847 and 1851, and in 1850 alone 660 were evicted from Barra. The reduced population in the Highlands (which began to decline in absolute numbers after 1851) gave the area some breathing space but did nothing to solve the underlying problems, or make those who remained any more resilient against adversity. The increasing trend to using the land for sport helped to provide some local work; but, paradoxically, large congested areas remained in areas such as Lewis, and the willingness of people to struggle through by using temporary migration to supplement crofting showed how tenacious the gaels' desire to occupy the land remained. Probably the most potent legacy was to make highlanders more politically conscious, generally mistrustful of landlords and more determined in future to resist any further erosion of their position.[19]

Even before the Church split, the social welfare system had been increasingly strained trying to cope with the emerging needs of an industrial society. Poor relief in Scotland had been designed for local communities to help them overcome temporary shortages in a subsistence economy, not for long bouts of unemployment in anonymous industrial towns. Income was expected to come from voluntary church givings, but by the 1830s most of the populous areas had come to rely mainly on local assessments. Even so, only a minority of parishes (some 239 out of 879) were formally assessed in 1839. Critics of the system said that it was arbitrary in its effects, that those administering it acted as judge and jury in deciding who should or should not be relieved, and that by failing to provide for those unemployed because of trade recessions, it constituted a serious danger to public health by making the population more subject to epidemics. While all this became increasingly clear in the 1830s, what is surprising is that in a decade of heightened political tension between the classes, so little sustained complaint came from below, from those most affected. This suggests that people perhaps expected social capital to be provided in other ways than by formal direct subsidies – in schools, public work schemes or communal temporary support. Perhaps, too, the social philosophy of the Scottish Enlightenment was too pervasive and persuasive to make people think that it could be challenged. By teaching that wealth came through the frugal attitudes of those likely to invest in growth, it had cultivated a thrift mentality that forced the individual look to himself and not to the public purse for support.

By 1840, however, it was obvious that something had to be done when whole towns like Paisley suddenly ceased to operate, and the government found itself forced to intervene. The General Assembly had produced a Report in 1839, aimed at reinforcing the Church's position as the main agent of local government, which claimed that the system, with its reliance on voluntary support, was still functioning effectively. However, it had to admit that the practice of assessment was spreading and its authors were clearly already uneasy. So, too, were an increasing number of medical men, who linked the soaring death rate in cities to the meagreness of the system. Recent research shows that W. P. Alison, Professor of Medicine at Edinburgh University, who undermined Chalmers' arguments for retaining the old system in a substantial pamphlet published in 1840, had already aired these views anonymously in *Blackwood's Magazine* in 1836.[20] Although Alison's concerns were the public health consequences of retaining the old system, his argument was basically a philosophical one, in which he demonstrated that the consequences of guaranteeing a basic level of subsistence to the population as predicted by Malthus were fanciful and unproven.

This was a real change in the prevailing intellectual mood. So, too, was the response of the government, guided by the Lord Advocate, Duncan McNeill, in its Scottish Poor Law Amendment Act of 1845. The General Assembly itself had asked for a public inquiry in May 1841 and in January 1843 (already before the Disruption took place) the government set up a Royal Commission. Its report is a curious document. Basically, it claimed that the old system was one which had always excluded the able-bodied, alimented only those who could not help themselves (the aged, orphaned and crippled) and was thus highly beneficial in maintaining the morale of the country. Throughout, however, it had to acknowledge that the 12 volumes of evidence from which it drew these conclusions constantly contradicted such assertions, and showed that the system was very much more flexible and so highly localised that it was impossible to speak of a 'national' or 'Scottish' poor law. Its main recommendations were to set up a Board of Supervision in Edinburgh which, to ensure that the existing law was carried out more effectively, would receive annual reports from a clerk appointed by the heritors and kirk sessions, with partly elected management committees wherever local assessments were levied.[21]

In 1845, the government took these rather hesitant proposals and stiffened them up considerably in the Poor Law Amendment Act, to ensure that in future not only would the system be more efficiently administered but that relief would be more adequate (not greater), and that applicants would be better able to enforce their claims. Far from being a half-hearted measure, the 1845 Act marked a real change of direction. Critics such as Alison were heartened to find that, even if it did not yet guarantee the able-bodied relief as in England, it went much further than the proposals in the Royal Commission.[22] What is significant about the reform of the Scottish poor law in 1845 is that it did not follow either the English Act of 1834 or the Irish Act of 1838. Instead, it tried to balance the localities with a central body, a Board of Supervision, which exercised general oversight and powers from Edinburgh. Along with this, local parochial boards, partly elected, were to be set up in each of the parishes immediately. These were to appoint a local Inspector of Poor who could only be dismissed by the Board in Edinburgh. Since he became criminally liable for the condition of each applicant, temporary relief was to be given out until a decision on the case was made. This increasingly forced parishes to assess themselves to ensure adequate funds, and by 1849 the number of taxed parishes had jumped to 644. It also became easier to appeal against local decisions to the Board of Supervision. The immediate effects of the Act in tackling the existing amount of underprovision were shown by the rise in the registered poor from about 2.8 per cent of the population to about 4.2 per cent by 1850. For the first time, a new administrative body to deal with modern conditions was set up in Edinburgh on the basis that decisions in such areas were best made according to local knowledge and circumstances. Those who wanted to keep the old system and reformers who wanted to alter it radically both agreed on one thing. Neither wanted a system run from some central board in London. Inevitably, such administrative devolution was bound to grow now that there was a body to which further powers could be added.[23]

These changes were a small but significant part of the national debate on how society should be run which came to a climax in these years. At the ordinary level Scotland, with its tradition of popular literacy, its many mechanics' institutes and its expanding press, provided a fertile market for influential writers such as J. R. McCulloch to popularise the lessons taught by the classical economists as to the 'iron laws' of supply and demand which operated in an industrialising society. These were: that material progress was part of a providential plan in which hard work and thrift brought its own reward; therefore, apprenticeship restrictions or strikes which might restrict this freedom were not only self-defeating but threatened the general welfare and flew in the face of nature. This reflected the fears of Ricardian economists who, at a more sophisticated level, were now concentrating on the processes which governed the distribution, as well as the growth of wealth. They saw, more clearly than Adam Smith had, that increases in population and higher wages and expectations would squeeze profits and encourage the rapid introduction of machinery to replace more costly labour. This, they argued, would lead to increasing conflict between the classes so that only the landed interest, protected by the Corn Laws, would benefit from the struggle for subsistence. Ricardo's solution was to remove the latter bottleneck by looking to an international division of labour through Free Trade and the removal of agricultural protection.

Food imports would help keep down the cost of living and dampen social antagonisms, while long-term education on these underlying laws of growth would finally convince the labouring population that their interests lay in supporting employers' capital ventures selling on a widening international marketplace.[24] Such views brought the great interests of commerce and land into increasing conflict. It was small wonder, therefore, that if the experts were engaged in heated discussion over the direction to be taken in response to the economic developments of the period, the reactions of those undergoing the traumas of change, the working classes, should appear to be spasmodic and lacking in consistency in these decades.

It is not surprising that, in these years, the trades unions found it difficult to develop a strong counter-view to this prevailing orthodoxy. They were baulked of political influence by the property restrictions on voting after 1832, and their ability to sustain their industrial strength was weak. Despite their great numbers, the handloom weavers had little control over entry and were too scattered to be able to bring combined pressure to bear in trying to stop the decline in their wages. The cotton spinners occupied a better strategic position since they were grouped inside factories, but their attempt, in a large and bitter strike in 1837, to prevent dilution through the introduction of new machinery failed. The sentencing of their leaders to transportation for seven years in 1838 caused a general loss of morale throughout the industrial areas, so that similar strikes among masons, colliers and ironworkers caused by the downturn of 1836–7 also soon collapsed.[25] Among trades such as the masons or the bakers, which had always been organised, gains made during periods of growth were even more quickly lost during such recessions, making it all the more difficult to regroup thereafter. In the growing engineering and metal trades of the west, the workshops and forges and shipyards were still small-scale concerns, so that disputes tended to be localised, usually ending in the employer's favour, as in shipyards like Denny's at Dumbarton.

The highly local and regional economies of Scotland also inhibited more general action. Craftsmen in textiles or engineering or traditional groups, such as carpenters in Edinburgh, Dundee or Aberdeen, had little in common with similar groups in the industrial west, and tended to look for support from other trades in the immediate locality. In coal and iron mining there were more consistent attempts to build up county organisations to maintain wage levels and working conditions through controlling output. A tradition of collective union action was gradually built up in episodes in 1817–18, 1824–5, 1830–2 and 1835–7. The rapid expansion in ironmaking, however, changed the nature of the industry and the new labour force constantly undermined the efforts of the traditional colliers. It was an uphill task to persuade the new men that their long-term interests lay in developing the frugal lifestyle necessary to sustain a well funded trade union when they lived in conditions which made such aspirations seem unattainable. In addition, united action remained very localised, the different structure and markets of the east of Scotland assocations discouraging the formation of a national body to exert combined pressure.

The wonder, indeed, is not so much that trades unions remained weak and cautious, despite the very real grievances of these years, as that they persisted and managed to survive in the face of such odds. There were some attempts at local joint action, in 1833 and 1838 and again in the 1840s, and these began to bear some fruit with the formal establishment of local trades councils in Glasgow and Edinburgh in the 1850s. The idea of forming a Scottish union had been mooted, too, among the miners ever since the early 1840s and began to be realised to some extent in the 1850s under the leadership of one of the most remarkable of Scottish Victorians, Alexander McDonald. A collier who saved in order to attend university and then gave up a comfortable teaching career to fight for the miners, who became financially independent by investing in coal companies, he combined in his person many of the apparent contradictions and shifting strategies of these years. Knowing the odds, he was never convinced that strikes were beneficial, always preferring negotiation, and he supported assisted emigration as a surer way of raising the value of labour at home.[26]

Working-class radicals also challenged the passive role assigned to them in prevailing economic and social theory by renewing their demands for further political reform. Economic uncertainties, plus the increasing conservatism of the Whig political leadership by the mid-1830s, sharpened the sense of working-class identity. Working-class radicals argued that labour was not a commodity and that wealth could lead to the dispossession of some and the benefit of others; consequently, these contending class interests needed to be balanced by greater political equality. The Chartist programme of 1838 provided them with a focus for these feelings. Building on existing radical centres, over 160 Chartist Associations were quickly formed by 1839, stretching from the north-east to the Borders, to petition for the six points. These reflected the differing radical traditions and economic mixtures in each locality. In Aberdeen, Chartism was led by traditional artisans with a long history, not so much of industrial conflict as of opposition to social privilege, who shared a great deal with the local middle classes in their aspirations for social betterment. In Dundee, Chartism was linked with the industrial grievances of its linen workers. In Glasgow and the west, its membership was more varied with a higher proportion of industrial workers and associated militancy. Overall, however, its leaders had a strong sense of the practicalities of the situation and the need for a long-haul strategy to improve the overall condition of the working classes. Local expertise enabled it to survive the disarray of the movement after the failure of that first phase in England, and to develop strong organisations of its own such as the Chartist Churches, of which there were over 20 by 1840. It produced its own newspapers, such as the *True Scotsman* (1838–43), the *Scottish Patriot* (1839–41) and the *Chartist Circular* (1839–42), as well as numerous co-operative, temperance and educational ventures and lecture tours.[27]

Despite the discouragement caused by successive failures at petitioning, the Chartist movement, therefore, proved remarkably persistent in Scotland, especially in the field of propaganda and in the boost it gave to self-help ventures such as the co-operative movement. It has been estimated that some 60 per cent of the local Chartist Associations founded in the first flush of enthusiasm in 1838 and 1839 in Scotland were still in existence providing focal points for further activities in the 1840s. Many of its leaders had been involved in previous radical agitations and they drew on this history in support of their claims. Just as some of the popular ballads composed for the Reform demonstrations in 1831 pointed to Baird and Hardie as forerunners of reform, they, too, saw themselves as continuing earlier struggles. Despite their emphasis on reason and self-help as the way to achieve their ends, the setting up of monuments in various localities to the victims of the 1820 Radical War by leading Scottish Chartists in 1847 suggests that they had no wish to disown their past. The political activists and egalitarians of the later eighteenth and early nineteenth centuries were often cited in their newspapers as 'proto-chartists'.[28] The experience that they gained from their efforts to promote the Charter was important in the longer term in helping to create a political tradition which was willing to make concessions while not abandoning its own history and interests. Although they failed to gain any of their specific demands by 1848, their activity and the way in which they presented their arguments had begun to persuade some contemporary clergymen and local political spokesmen to pay attention to working-class grievances. By the early 1850s they had opened doors which had seemed closed in the middle 1830s, so that middle-class spokesmen were now more willing to take up the cause of further franchise reform knowing that they had popular backing behind them which was firmly rooted in the localities. Among the working population as a whole, many more people became politically aware as a result of Chartist propaganda efforts and gained increased confidence in their ability to run the organisations needed to justify their claims. They were realistic enough by the 1850s, too, to see that their best hopes for electoral reform lay in supporting the Liberals, but this was always conditional on their interests being best served by such an alliance. If that belief should ever waver, as it did in the 1870s and 1880s, so too would that alliance.[29]

Scottish politics in these years were shaped by the ecclesiastical and commercial concerns of the groups who had gained the vote in 1832. The election results (see Table 2.1) show that a period of permanent Liberal

*Table 2.1    Election results* (totals in brackets).

| Year | Liberal | | Conservative | |
|------|--------|----------|--------|----------|
|      | Burghs | Counties | Burghs | Counties |
| 1832 | 22 | 21 (43) | 1 | 9 (10) |
| 1835 | 22 | 16 (38) | 1 | 14 (15) |
| 1837 | 22 | 11 (33) | 1 | 19 (20) |
| 1841 | 21 | 10 (31) | 2 | 20 (22) |
| 1847 | 22 | 11 (33) | 1 | 19 (20) |
| 1852 | 22 | 11 (33) | 1 | 19 (20) |
| 1857 | 23 | 15 (38) | – | 15 (15) |
| 1859 | 23 | 15 (38) | – | 15 (15) |
| 1865 | 23 | 19 (42) | – | 11 (11) |

dominance and Conservative minority began in 1832 which was never seriously threatened until the later years of the century. This was based on the former's strength in the burgh constituencies, virtually all of which they held in unbroken sequence right up to the third Reform Act of 1884–5. Only Falkirk Burghs (which they won in 1841, 1847 and 1852) gave the Conservatives any sort of consistent support, and then only because of the local influence of the Bairds, the ironmasters, who were free traders. Conservative strength, such as it was, was confined to the counties.[30] Much of this was due to the gratitude felt towards the Liberals for having reformed the electoral system to bring it in line with the rest of the country, as well as resentment towards the Scottish Conservatives for having resisted change up to the bitter end. Such feelings were bound to subside in time, however, and new issues also played a part in determining the longer-term pattern. By the middle 1830s the Liberals were looking rather jaded and the Conservatives were beginning to win back some of the ground that they had lost, strengthening their position significantly in the counties. Natural deference on the part of the new county voters, especially the £50 tenants, had something to do with this, but so, too, had the twists and turns of the church question and the growing agitation to abolish the Corn Laws. These handicapped both parties in different ways, so that by 1850 the old Whig and Tory leaders had had to concede much ground to the new forces emerging in Scottish society.

The Whigs, whose belief in their right to rule and be deferred to was equal to that of the Tories, found their actions coming under increasing scrutiny from the Dissenters. Ever since 1832 these had been organising their new voting power in the constituencies and in 1834 had formed a Scottish Central Board of Dissenters to make sure that the links between church and state were ended, not strengthened. This was part of their general campaign for civil and religious liberties and went with support for the rational reform of existing institutions and the spread of Free Trade principles. Starting with the Leith by-election in 1834, Whig candidates found themselves challenged on their attitude to current ecclesiastical issues. The tenderness which the Grey administration appeared to display in its proposals to reform the Established Church in Ireland also roused their suspicions. So, too, did the government's temporising attitude towards the evangelicals as they sought government help in their schemes to reform and strengthen the church. Some of this resulted in a drop in support for Liberal candidates in the 1837 general election as Dissenters abstained.[31]

Conversely, the Conservatives' determination to uphold the institutions of church and state helped them to recover some of the ground lost over Reform. Peel's reputation began to grow among urban churchmen, who welcomed his support for their policy of church extension during his visit to the west of Scotland in 1836 and 1837. This gave a much needed fillip to his party's fortunes. By 1837 the Conservatives had doubled the seats that they held in 1832 to 20 and by 1841 to 22, including two burgh constituencies. More significantly, their hold was now too solid in 16 of the counties for the Liberals to wish to contest them. There was no reason why the Conservatives should not have continued to consolidate their hold in their natural strongholds in the counties where they had strong support from great territorial magnates such as Buccleuch, Aberdeen, Queensberry and others. However, as noted earlier, Peel's growing reservations about the direction being taken by the church reformers in Scotland, and his determination not to support them until they should act within the law as defined by the courts, brought him into increasing collision with the Non-Intrusionists after 1839. When he became Prime Minister in 1841 his rejection of their Claim of Right and the subsequent Disruption unleashed the bitter resentment of the new Free Church against those they felt should have been their defenders against the attacks of the voluntaries. The refusal of some landlords to provide sites for the new church in rural areas, particularly in the Highlands, reinforced their antipathy towards what they now regarded as the party of the landed classes and the Establishment they had just quit. What made Free Church opposition particularly damaging to the Conservatives (and also to some extent to the older Whig elements within the Liberals) was that it added respectability to the Dissenters, its leading members having recently been pillars of the Establishment; but, more than that, being strong in the counties as well as in the towns, it swelled the potential anti-Conservative vote further. Altogether, in organisation and numbers they formed a formidable new voting bloc. The signs of this were already there in the 1841 election, when Non-Intrusion became a defining issue for all candidates in Scotland and where, in contrast to the large gains that the Conservatives made in England, they won only 22 of the 53 seats.[32]

The Whigs had also been less than helpful to the Non-Intrusionists, not only because they did not want to alienate their own radical support at a time when their parliamentary majority was becoming ever more precarious in 1839 and 1840, but because they too were temperamentally just as unhappy with the character and pretensions of this new urban, middle-class driven force as were the Conservatives. However, they were more accommodating than Peel and willing to accept new alliances to keep the Conservatives out, especially when Free Church leaders like Candlish began to forge consituency deals with his erstwhile voluntary enemies among the Seceders at the end of 1846, in preparation for the coming general election. These resulted in a reduction of the absolute hold of the old guard Whigs within Scottish Liberalism; most spectacularly, in the unseating of T. B. Macaulay in Edinburgh and the ousting of the two Whiggish Liberals in Glasgow, and their replacement by Dissenters in the general election of 1847. What helped to consolidate these movements was not only the determination of the Free churchmen to hit back at the Conservatives but Peel's decision in 1845 to increase, and now make permanent, the grant for the upkeep of the Roman Catholic College at Maynooth. This provided common ground for both the Seceders, who opposed it as further strengthening the detested principle of state endowment of religion, and the Free churchmen, who hated it because it not only promoted Roman Catholicism but gave it the government support which had been denied to their own church extension pleas.[33]

The centrality of religion in public debate was not simply due to a preoccupation with points of doctrine by the shopkeeping classes who had been enfranchised in 1832. It was also a focus for a whole range of other social, economic and political grievances which could equally be regarded as moral issues. Being a Seceder went with being against the status quo on grounds of conscience. Seceders of all hues felt themselves second-class citizens by definition in relation to the Established Church because of the privileged position that it enjoyed as compared with their own brand of religion. Edinburgh's Annuity Tax, levied for the maintenance of the city's ministers, was one such grievance, a burden borne by everyone for the benefit of one particular section of the community, just like the Corn Laws. Such protection was easily linked to the economic as well as the moral distress of the 1830s and 1840s. Protecting the landlords hurt industry and did not feed the hungry: protecting the church did not visibly lessen the level of urban crime and squalor and class antagonism. There was often little to distinguish Dissenters from Churchmen in terms of wealth and respectability, but the formers' rise to prosperity had often been more recent and the risks they had taken might easily fail if their profits declined. Since food played a large part in determining costs in wages, they saw the very landed interest which supported the Church of Scotland having its agricultural profits protected by law. In return, since the ministers' stipends were tied to average grain price levels, they saw these twin establishment pillars thus reinforcing each other in apparent self-interest. The landed classes, who had supported the Moderates in controlling the Church, were among the staunchest upholders of the old politics and the fiercest opponents of enfranchising the classes who were strong among the Seceders. Even when the vote had been won, the old Tory interests now seemed to be using their control over their tenants in the counties to nullify its effects. Therefore, they argued, more voters were needed along with the ballot to make the electorate less amenable to such manipulation.[34]

Religion was thus a determining line along which political allegiances split. The Church was suspected of not having changed its spots and, therefore, of being opposed to further reform. To those outside of it, radicalism in religion almost always went with radicalism in politics. In time, the Conservatives might have hoped that their fortunes would improve with the eventual revival of the Established Church. What prevented this was the impact of the Anti-Corn Law agitation. Support for the general principle of Free Trade was widespread in Scotland and stretched far beyond the ranks of dissent. Like the Church question, this posed problems for the leadership in both the Liberal and Conservative parties, for the latter more than for the former. The fact that it was Peel who had to handle the question of Repeal of the Corn Laws in 1846 proved too much for his party to overcome in Scotland. Equally the whiggish elements within the Liberals were forced to give ground and become more radical on this issue.[35]

Scotland proved fruitful ground for the Anti-Corn Law activists because it was already well prepared for agitation on the issue. Protests at the passing of the Corn Law of 1815 had been pretty widespread and the issue became prominent again in 1833 once the Reform Bill had been passed. Organisations were formed in the major cities to make propaganda on the question, pamphlets were issued, meetings and demonstrations held and town councils, for example, were persuaded to condemn the Corn Laws. The movement was well led in Scotland by radicals like William Weir, editor of the *Glasgow Argus*, and John Hill Burton and John Tait in Edinburgh. By 1837 Weir was advocating the formation of a Central Association to coordinate local activity and put pressure on MPs. Thus, when the Anti-Corn Law League was formally organised in Manchester in March 1838 there were ready-made organisations in all the major towns in Scotland, with experienced leaders and much of the initiative in the argument. The Whigs found their preference for gradual reform overtaken by such pressure. Already by 1839 there were at least 13 Scottish newspapers openly advocating Free Trade. Peel's decision in 1842 to introduce a sliding scale of duties was welcomed not only by the *Scotsman*, which by then had accepted the principle of total repeal – only differing from the League over how soon this could be done – but, more importantly, by the Conservative-leaning *Glasgow Herald*, the voice of the commercial classes in the west.[36]

There are several reasons why the Anti-Corn Law movement should have been so successful in moulding Scottish political opinion. One is that the issue had for long been a central part of the radical programme.

There was a long history of popular resistance to measures that seemed to exacerbate the periodic grain shortages due to bad harvests. In addition, the argument that greater productivity should lead to cheaper food chimed in very well with the prevailing classical economic orthodoxy. Those arguing for protection were swimming against the current intellectual tide in Scotland. Free Trade was an assertion of a way of living in which status was earned, not inherited by drawing on 'unearned' rent: it was the market which allowed all to progress, not the protection of group interest. It was, thus, a policy which appealed to a wide spectrum of opinion in the urban areas among those who had gained a political say after 1832. The fact that its proponents in Scotland saw it as part of a wider package of reform which included some further widening of the franchise, the secret ballot and the modernisation of the country's institutions made it appeal not only to the middle classes but also to the working-class radicals. Very important was the way in which the League could mobilise the growing body of Dissent in its favour. Men such as the Rev. Ralph Wardlaw, leader of the Glasgow Congregationalists, Dr Heugh of the Secession and John Wigham of the Quakers in Edinburgh all threw their moral weight behind the movement. When a great meeting of Dissenters was organised in Manchester in 1841 to show their support for the movement, Duncan McLaren, the leading layman in the United Secession, followed this up with a similar demonstration in Edinburgh in January 1842, attended by nearly 700 voluntary ministers, over half of whom were from the Secession and Relief churches. In the same month a great Anti-Corn Law conference was organised in Glasgow by a leading local whig businessman, Walter Buchanan, with delegates from 26 areas. Clearly the publicity, the initiative and the popular mood was overwhelmingly on the side of the Free Traders in Scotland.[37]

Peel's abolition of the Corn Laws in 1846, therefore, tore a great hole in the Conservative party in Scotland. The protectionists found themselves reduced to a small rump. In truth, there had been little opposition from either the farming classes or the Conservatives in Scotland to the campaign being waged by the League. This was partly due to the fact that grain played very little part in the prosperity of Scottish agriculture outside of Midlothian and Fife. Thus, attempts at counter-organisation were very late in starting and, when they did in 1844, generally lacked the drive of the Anti-Corn Law movement. It was partly due, too, to the fact that many of the Conservative MPs representing the Scottish counties shared Peel's views. It is remarkable that in the vote to repeal the Corn Laws the English counties went 107 to 25 against Peel, whereas the Scottish county MPs went 14 to 10 for Peel. While the Conservatives appeared to hold on quite well with 20 seats at the general election of 1847, compared with 22 in 1841, their buoyancy had gone. They contested far fewer seats, leaving the Liberals easy walkovers, while 12 of their county seats were held by Peelites. In the longer term these tended to drift towards the Liberals, with the Derbyite true-blues reduced to a few scattered holdings in the northeast and the Borders. In the burghs it became almost impossible for anyone not wholeheartedly committed to Free Trade to stand,[38] and many burgh seats remained uncontested by the Conservatives until the later 1860s and 1870s. Finally, current events seemed to give Free Trade the authority of an economic truth. Protection had not prevented the north and north-west of Scotland from experiencing a terrible famine, while Free Trade gained all the credit for the burst of prosperity and growth that marked the years after 1850. Although the Conservatives still stood at the same level in 1852 as in 1847, five of their seats were still held by Peelites and the others were drifting to Conservative-Liberals, so that their 15 seats in 1857 is the truer picture of their plight after the party split of 1846.[39]

Thus Free Trade, like Free Church, had profoundly altered the nature of Scottish politics by the 1850s. It was no longer a sign of political extremism, as it had been in 1833 and 1834, to call for immediate repeal of the Corn Laws. The electorate became less deferential as issues of conscience came to the fore. New radical elements became more confident, challenging the old guard leadership and winning for themselves some say in decision-making. While the richer merchants and manufacturers managed to retain overall control of the Liberal party, after 1850 they had to accommodate themselves to these new forces, becoming more sympathetic to some further extension of the franchise and willing to consider measures to modernise the country's insitutions. They also had to take account of the great body of Dissent represented by the United Presbyterians (formed in 1847 from the union of the United Secession and the Relief Church) and the Free Church.

These events had the effect of defining Scotland's political identity in terms of almost total support for the Liberal party. After 1847, Scotland became virtually a one-party state. Its Liberalism reflected the ethos of betterment through individual effort as prescribed by contemporary classical economic theory. Scottish Liberalism was not particularly noted for its emphasis on ameliorative measures to protect commun-

ities in the process of transition. However, it was concerned with the
workings of social structures and increasingly anxious to create more
efficient institutions for the government of society. But these, it felt, had
to be devised in conformity with what seemed best for local conditions,
in accordance with local values, and not be imposed through an increasingly centralised British state. By the 1850s, Scottish society was
taking on a shape politically that continued to distinguish it from the
rest of Britain as much as its geography, social structure and institutions
did. It wanted its growing contribution to Britain's greatness recognised and its institutions modernised through closer links with English
ideas and practices; but it also wanted to control the pace of this growing
unification so that it did not lose sight of the values on which its progress
was based. Its rejection of the Conservative party was not so much a
rejection of conservative values as a rejection of values associated with
English squires and parsons. Its Liberalism was an assertion of an
identity which had been formed out of the contentions experienced by
its ecclesiastical, economic and institutional interests before 1850.

# 3

## NORTH BRITAIN: 1850–86

The sustained economic growth which lasted until the later 1870s created a general feeling of prosperity in Victorian Scotland. Employment opportunities in the expanding metal and extractive industries more than compensated for the slowing down in cotton spinning and the sharp decline in handloom weaving. The Clyde's reputation for technological innovation was making it the main supplier of the new iron-hulled ships and advanced boilers. Thus, as world trade expanded, demanding faster and larger ships and corresponding fuel economies, it went from launching about a third to just over a half of all British tonnage between 1860 and 1870. By the latter date, half of all men employed in British shipbuilding worked on Clydeside. By 1870, too, output of pig iron had soared to over 1 million tons, that of coal had doubled since 1854 to nearly 15 million tons, and a flourishing malleable iron industry was now in place alongside the traditional cast iron sector. All of this meant enormous commercial expansion throughout central Scotland. In other sectors, specialised textile production and bleaching and dyeing continued to flourish, as did the mighty chemical industry, which found new outlets in the growing metal developments. At the same time, the increasing trade in bulk products, plus the outbreak of a series of wars on the continent and in the United States, stimulated demand for coarse sacking and raised the jute and linen output of Dundee to new heights. These foreign discords also ensured that the increasingly sophisticated agricultural sector faced little challenge after the removal of protective duties in 1846, while its varied output made it well placed to supply the growing market being created by manufacturing.[1]

As a result of the above developments, society underwent greater changes in the second half of the century than it had in the preceding turbulent decades. The redistribution of population was more marked, urbanisation was more widespread, and people's lives were increasingly dominated by the working disciplines of heavy industry as Clydeside became a great world centre in shipbuilding and engineering. Yet, paradoxically, the sense of strain was not so great as it had been earlier in the century. The great questions of church and state, of economy and society had been settled for the time being in the struggles surrounding the Disruption, the Corn Laws and Chartism. These had often involved a desire to go back to an older world of work and communal relations. After 1850, however, the public had become used to change, and there was a general acceptance of the new factory civilisation and the need to develop within it. What the latter would entail lay behind the first stirrings in the country's search for its modern identity.

A sense of the past had always existed at the popular level: traditional airs and songs and references to historical precedents in figures like Wallace or the Covenanters figured regularly at public demonstrations, while local customs and associations continued to be nourished in the columns of the provincial press.[2] Among the upper and literary classes, too, both the spread of historical clubs and the religious controversies in the first half of the century had fuelled a lively debate on the country's past.[3] Now, more practical considerations about how the country should be governed were raising questions about its place within the United Kingdom. Parliament was playing a larger role in meeting the needs of a modernising Britain, but the Scots felt that their interests tended to go by default there and, consequently, that they had less control over the pace of change. Their lack of political weight plus the different legal situation often meant that the Lord Advocate could not get parliamentary time for separate Scottish bills. The alternatives were the unsatisfactory tacking on of Scottish clauses to legislation designed for England, which was often found to be inoperable in Scotland, or general legislation designed for the whole kingdom (which might mean some form of unwanted control from London, especially if conflicts existed over which priorities and strategies to adopt). The responses to the industrialisation affecting both England and Scotland were bound eventually to lead to some standardisation in administration. After all, why should general questions of health need separate answers if typhus or tuberculosis knew no national boundaries? However, in these and even more sensitive areas such as education there was a need to allow for local conditions and traditions in tackling such matters. A good example of the need for new health legislation in Scotland was the defective state of its laws regarding nuisance. No matter how many regulations local authorities might lay down to control environmental conditions and prevent epidemics, it was very hard to define legally what consituted a nuisance in Scotland. A habit sanctioned by prescription, such as dumping sewage on fields next to towns, could become a property right after some years and be very difficult to prevent except through expensive local litigation. Other vital areas where the basis was different were the laws governing housing and land tenure, and education.

By 1850 there was a general feeling that a number of issues particular to Scotland needed greater attention than its hard-pressed Lord Advocate and its few MPs with their various interests could give, such as the condition of large parts of the Highlands and of its industrial population, as well as the functioning of its educational system. The recent ecclesiastical upheavals added to the feeling of government neglect. The growth of the popular press in this period not only provided a local context for the discussion of such issues: the speedier exchange of views made possible now by the railway and the electric telegraph also brought the opinions of the English press before the Scottish public more readily than ever before and, when these appeared to be sometimes too critical or ill-informed about Scottish issues and sentiments, they created further irritation.[4]

These discontents led to a re-examination of Scotland's Union with England – not to break it, but to make it work more effectively – and they found some expression in the short-lived National Association for the Vindication of Scottish Rights, established in 1853. This attracted a great deal of support from the outset. It held a series of well attended meetings in Edinburgh and Glasgow and other towns and received, on the whole, a positive response from a substantial section of the Scottish press to the issues it raised. Its *Address to the People of Scotland* (1853), which sold widely, acknowledged the Union of 1707 but wanted to improve it to take account of the times. It deplored the assumed incorporation of Scottish institutions and symbols into those of England and listed real financial grievances. Scotland currently contributed nearly £6 million to the Treasury but received comparatively little in return, whereas Ireland, for much less, received a great deal more. There was no government support for public institutions in Edinburgh as there was in London and Dublin, nor for its universities, and almost no military or naval spending or help in building much needed harbours. To defend its interests, therefore, it demanded an increase in the number of its MPs (to match its increased population and wealth) together with a Secretary of State to articulate domestic concerns inside government. The leaders of the Association were mainly outsiders in Scottish public life, representing a variety of often conflicting interests. At the forefront were the historical novelists, John and James Grant, with their protests over the misuse of heraldic symbols denying Scotland's ancient nationhood, Tories such as the Earl of Eglinton and Sir Archibald Alison, and the poet W. E. Aytoun, as well as radicals like Patrick Dove, the political theorist and journalist, and Duncan McLaren and Charles Cowan, respectively Lord Provost and MP for Edinburgh. Its winding up by 1855 indicates how easily such a movement could lose its momentum when overtaken by wider events such as the Crimean War.[5]

Nevertheless, it would be a mistake to think that the issues it had raised would also fade away quickly. Far from being ephemeral, these had a long history, and their articulation by the National Association was just the latest, although the most organised to date, of a series of such complaints. In 1825 Sir John Sinclair, in his *Analysis of the Statistical Account of Scotland*, had expressed precisely the same concern about government failure to treat Scotland in accordance with its contribution to the national exchequer, especially when compared with Ireland, which obtained more MPs, more money and generally more consideration from parliament than law-abiding, industrious Scots did. Soon after 1832, whig reformers like Francis Jeffrey and Henry Cockburn were becoming disillusioned about the lack of consideration for Scottish business, the latter in 1836 calling for a Scottish Secretary instead of an overworked Lord Advocate to keep the Scottish MPs in line (the reintroduction of a more representative system of 'management'?). Arguments for a federal scheme of local parliaments which would allow localities to respond to change while leaving the supreme parliament to get on with the overall tasks of national government had already appeared in a pamphlet published in Glasgow in 1844.[6]

The Scots' sense of being British, which was based on sharing a common language and religious history with England, was stronger than any sense of particularism. But if Scotland was 'North Britain', was there a 'South Britain' and, indeed, what was 'Britain'? The answers here varied in emphasis depending on whether they were viewed from London or from within Scotland. Most Scots, including many who felt some sympathy for the views of the National Association, had no desire to cut themselves off from English culture or participation in English life. It would have been surprising had they done so, especially when the age which had produced Dickens, Tennyson, Thackery and the Brontës had given them so many shared icons. Indeed, they often described themselves as English when taking pride in national achievements. At the same time they wanted to reinforce the connection by having their contribution to the United Kingdom given fuller acknowledgment. Such apparent incongruities can be seen in the career of Victorians such as David Livingstone, lauded for his British role in Africa yet inspired to it by a background which was peculiarly Scottish in its blending of science and religion.[7] It is not surprising, therefore, that Scottish public opinion should reveal so many apparent inconsistencies in its attempts to explore these issues: a welcome for English models which would help it to modernise itself, but a belief, too, that its own progressive values, derived from the Enlightenment and the Reformation, had also played a vital part in making Britain into a great power; resentment at the assumption that Britain consisted solely of an England in which the Scots were subsumed, combined with a desire to share in the culture and economic opportunities made possible by their union with England. To a certain extent it could be said that they were more consciously unionist than the English were. Those who now dominated Scottish life, after all, attributed their social and political emancipation to the Union with England, and their political loyalty was to the British institutions which had given them Reform in 1832, not to the feudal institutions of the Scottish past. Nevertheless, they did not want their particular mixture of social and cultural values to be taken for granted.

From the centre, the situation seemed much more clear-cut and such psychological, cultural and historical nuances less significant. *The Times* dismissed the Scottish agitation of the 1850s by arguing that there were no barriers to Scottish advancement in an England in which former notions of nationality had been replaced with a superior 'conception of a United Kingdom, nay of a British Empire'. It thus ironically made the Scottish Rights case in its unconscious assumption that Britishness consisted in sharing the values of those who ruled the Empire from England. Interestingly, the most effective answer to *The Times*' case came from someone who did not start from a unionist viewpoint, the Highland land reformer, John Murdoch. He pointed out that it depended on who decided what values should prevail, observing that when, in the eyes of *The Times*, their virtues of enterprise, perseverance and integrity were used in the service of the prevailing ruling groups, they commended Scots to high office; but, when they were used to claim rights for themselves or their country they were regarded as 'foibles to be sneered at'.[8] Murdoch was arguing a wider case about power and the use of resources, based on the view that the ordinary people throughout Britain had a common interest in amending a bargain which in 1707 had guaranteed the rights of the governors but not of the people below – a view which was still very much a minority one in the 1850s.

The unionist character of much of this mid-century nationalism and some of its less often recognised links with the working classes can be detected in the hugely popular meetings held in Scotland in support of the foreign liberation movements of this period in Hungary and in Italy. At these, ex-chartists such as James Moir and John McAdam were able to join with middle-class Liberals to identify with figures like Kossuth, Garibaldi and Mazzini, and present their struggles against the Habsburgs and the Papacy as fights for civil and religious freedoms which they themselves already enjoyed as Britons. Outside of London it was areas like Scotland which gave the greatest support to these causes. Men like McAdam saw themselves not as struggling to break the links uniting Britain, but as exporting freedoms that they already enjoyed, and for the winning of which they wanted some recognition.[9] The significant link here is that of the cult of William Wallace as national patriot. Nationalist agitation in the later 1850s and 1860s was sustained by the campaign to erect a national Wallace memorial and McAdam was active in raising funds and supporting this agitation. McAdam saw the struggle to extend the franchise at home as part of these popular movements in Europe, and drew parallels between Wallace and figures like Garibaldi. Popular revolts in Europe against Catholic Habsburgs and Papal rule tapped much support in the atmosphere created in Scotland by the Maynooth Grant, the strident opposition to the restoration of the Catholic hierarchy in England in 1850, and the recent large scale famine migrations from Ireland. However incongruously, this medieval figure was projected as the symbol of everyman's struggle for freedom and of the virtues of British Protestantism now being exported abroad. Once again, such movements did not spring up suddenly in the 1850s but were part of an older tradition. In 1818, in the afterglow of British victory over Napoleonic France, there had been similar moves to set up a Wallace monument in Glasgow to symbolise Scotland's progressive values.[10]

The practical issues raised by the Scottish Rights movement, such as the need for more MPs and a Scottish Secretary, were increasingly taken up, in 1858 and again in the later 1860s, by newer MPs like Duncan McLaren who wanted to shift political control away from the lawyers and landed interests in Edinburgh towards the needs of the modern urban Scotland that had emerged. Nor did the decline of the National Association by 1855 end the debate on questions of Scottish influence in parliament, the pace of modernisation and the values to be adopted therein. A highly political argument was going on both within Scotland and at the same time within parliamentary opinion at Westminster over the reform of the country's educational system. Behind this lay the wider cultural considerations sparked off by the growth of an urban society struggling to overcome the environmental deficits of rapid industrialisation and poor housing. An increasing number of voices began to argue that only by reinvigorating their national institutions and civilising their lapsed masses, amongst whom they included the great numbers of Catholic Irish, could the progressive values which had propelled Scotland to the forefront be sustained.

Valiant attempts were being made by mid-century to make up earlier deficiencies in provision and thus maintain the principles of a public educational system.[11] The trouble was that growth in the system was haphazard and had not always been directed to where it was most needed, so that many were still left unprovided for. Since 1839 some help had come from the Privy Council Committee on Education through grants, first to build and then to staff additional schools, and this intervention should have presented no difficulties in a country in which the state was expected to play a major part in the provision of education. However, its policy of restricting such aid to a minimum provision of the three Rs to the labouring classes was regarded as a threat to the all-through Scottish tradition which provided some teaching of higher subjects in order to link the ordinary schools with the universities.[12] In addition, the basic framework of parish schools, controlled by the Church of Scotland, with the masters subject to a religious test, no longer reflected the diversity of contemporary society. The conflicting interests involved made it difficult to find some common ground on which to build. The Church of Scotland wanted to retain its position as the national provider and mounted a vigorous campaign to gather support for its claims both in Scotland and England. The Free Church wanted to see its rival's control ended, but was split between those who wanted to join a more effective national system and those who wanted to go on accepting Privy Council grants for its own schools. The voluntaries, with their strict views on the separation of church and state, wanted a national system but no public money spent on religious instruction. A National Education Association set up in 1850 advocated a secular system. No one seems to have seriously considered how the Episcopalians and Roman Catholics might fit in.

With such internal strains it is small wonder that little was achieved before 1872. Successive attempts in parliament – two private bills in 1850 and 1851, followed by more official attempts by the Lord Advocate in 1854, 1855 and 1856 – gathered growing support from the majority of Scottish MPs, but were defeated by the greater number of English and Irish MPs who either did not want to see the powers of the Church of Scotland reduced or the principles of public education settled in Scotland before they had been thrashed out in England. This 'thwarting' of Scottish political opinion was much resented, and was seen as justifying some of the charges of second-class treatment made by the National Association in 1853. However, many of the difficulties in the way of a successful solution came from the ecclesiastical divisions which already existed inside the Scotland of the 1850s. The abortive bills all aimed at scrapping the religious tests and extending the parish system into one which was truly national, with a central education board in Edinburgh to oversee the system and partly elected local boards to determine the type of education, including religious instruction, thought to be acceptable. However, the small amount of religious education to be allowed was too much for the voluntaries but too little for the Church of Scotland; the Free Church hoped to save money on maintaining its own schools by reducing the Church of Scotland's control over the parish schools, while the secularists wanted no religious formularies at all; finally, many landowners saw no reason why the provision of extra schools should be put on the rates.[13]

In the 1850s and 1860s, advances in scientific knowledge, greater historical insights and contact with other societies through trade and travel led both to a more liberal outlook and at the same time a determination not to endanger the foundations of the new civilisation that was emerging. The main threat seemed to come from within the towns where large sections of the population appeared to live lives outwith the normal bounds of church, school and regular employment. These needed to be disciplined and encouraged into more civilised ways. The Lord Advocate had sounded this note in the education debates: 'while wealth was multiplying there was at the same time growing up a barbarian race in our cities'.[14] It found an echo in the more coercive licensing measures adopted in the larger towns to control the drink trade, which were eventually enshrined in the Forbes Mackenzie Act of 1853, which reduced opening hours (and also encouraged law-breaking and increased clandestine drinking).[15] More generally, these decades witnessed a determined effort to bring some order into urban areas, the needs of which had long outstripped those envisaged by the reformers in the 1833 legislation. The 1862 General Police Act enabled any populous area down to a minimum now of 700 inhabitants to adopt the powers needed for adequate town government and public health. A total of 185 towns, 84 of them non-burghs, took advantage of its provisions (now codified in the light of the experience gained from the 1833 and 1850 Police Acts and the 1856 Nuisance Act) to provide themselves with pavements, lighting, regulations for housebuilding and water supplies, producing the typical Victorian urban landscape of baronial town halls, regular paved streets lined with rows of stone tenements, shops and parks.[16] The larger towns such as Glasgow, Edinburgh, Dundee and Greenock, with their particular problems in housing and health, adopted specific Police and Improvement Acts to allow them to clear away congested and insanitary slum areas, enforce building regulations, improve water supplies, and build model lodging houses, wash-houses and municipal gas schemes. Besides cleaning up the environment, appointing medical officers and creating a boom in artisan housing in the 1860s and 1870s, such acts included a fair degree of social coercion. City centre 'Improvement' schemes demolished the worst plague spots, clearing more people in a decade than the most ruthless of Highland landlords had done – some 3000 people in Edinburgh and around 30 000 in Glasgow between 1867 and 1877 – and forcing them to 'flit' to nearby areas, which soon became just as congested. To contain the problem, Glasgow, and then Edinburgh and Dundee, resorted to 'ticketing' houses below a certain size, detailing the maximum numbers allowed to sleep in them and harrassing their inhabitants by regular inspections. Such actions were based on the theory that the respectable workers would make provision for themselves and that individual inadequacy explained why those who could not, or would not, do so found themselves in the worst areas.[17] Unsurprisingly, it did little to improve the slum dweller's morale or improve the already appalling standards of housing congestion. In spite of these schemes, housing conditions failed to improve; in 1871 a quarter of the population lived in single-ends (one-room houses) while another 38 per cent lived in a room and kitchen (two-room houses). The resulting overcrowding levels, of 54 per cent of the population living more than two to a room, obviously concealed wide variations, between the elderly widow living on her own and the crowded colliers' rows with their additions of lodgers. Towns such as Coatbridge had densities as high as the city of New York, but the ironmasters who dominated them fought off adopting burgh status until the 1880s. Smaller coastal towns such as Crail or Girvan seemed less pressurised only because they had more space around them.

Similar attempts to meet social pressures through self-reliance and voluntary help can be traced in the way in which the poor law was administered. In the 1850s the aim was to make sure that adequate relief was given, and by 1868 the amounts spent on the poor and the numbers relieved reached their peak. Thereafter, however, the policy imposed by the Board of Supervision was one of economy. The poorhouse was to be offered as a test of genuineness of need, to weed out the undeserving so that resources could be targeted towards the deserving poor. If the poorhouse offer was refused, then there were no grounds for appeal against inadequate relief. By the early 1860s, too, the discretionary power of the local parochial boards to relieve the temporarily unemployed had been declared illegal. Nevertheless, from what is known of the working of the parochial boards in the most populous Scottish county, Lanarkshire, a great deal of effort was made to continue to treat the poor according to local custom and knowledge, and to ignore too much direction from the centre. By 1878, the Board itself was having to admit the practice of some boards in allowing able-bodied men who were starving to be medically certified as sick.[18] Overall, however, there was little uniformity in practice between the various boards, and the main concern of the ratepayers and the few heritors who dominated them was to make every effort to keep the rates down. The feckless and those who could not cope were given up as hopeless, and the old or sick received the minimum. What is surprising is that during the trade depressions of the later 1850s and the 1860s there was so little protest by working men or expectation of public help except in the form of philanthropic or public subscription schemes. Their concern seemed to be to get back to work as quickly as possible, in the expectation that the trade cycle would once again pick up and revive demand for the country's products. Perhaps the enormous number of voluntary agencies now springing up to offer some form of temporary assistance helped blunt the edge of poverty among the better organised and more articulate. In Glasgow alone by 1900 there were over 500 societies in operation, which included 45 mortifications and bequests, 152 charitable societies, 201 trade and friendly societies, 13 clan associations and 58 evangelistic associations, many of them offering help to their members.[19]

In the educational sphere, a few changes were accomplished. In 1861, the religious tests for schoolmasters were finally abolished. Growing pressure from the professional and middle classes for the universities to respond to their changing needs led to some of the reforms recommended in the Royal Commission of 1826–30, such as making them more accountable and providing more specialised studies and more encouragement to graduation, being enacted in 1858. There was some acknowledgement here of the distinctive nature of the educational system in Scotland. Other reforms, such as introducing a qualifying entrance examination and thus raising the age of the students, were left aside, however, for any changes here would involve changes in the school curriculum. In the latter, proposals to introduce a more stringent system of payment by results in 1862 aroused widespread opposition because they seemed to threaten the teaching of higher subjects in the parish schools. These were then suspended until a Commission (1864–8) under the Duke of Argyll had investigated the educational situation more fully, and here again this seemed to acknowledge that Scottish education had to be treated differently.

Amongst other things, the Argyll Commission recommended that the national system with its links from parish and burgh schools to university should be preserved, but that the overall provision and quality of education should be improved under the guidance of an Education Board sitting in Edinburgh. A bill to build up the system on these lines failed in 1869, but when an Education Act was finally passed in 1872 (after the English Act of 1870) it preserved several features, in response to public opinion in Scotland, which continued to differentiate the system from that in England. Schooling was to become compulsory immediately for all children between 5 and 13 years. Effective education was to be provided by local school boards, popularly elected, to which all the parish and burgh schools were to be transferred. From the start, therefore, the principle of public provision was made truly effective, whereas in England the voluntary church schools were allowed ten years in which to make up any deficiencies in provision.[20]

The Act has not received a great deal of praise in recent years from historians. It has been criticised for the emphasis it put – like its English counterpart – on the elementary, to the detriment of the higher branches traditionally taught in Scottish schools which kept the path open, in theory at any rate, to university. Although a separate Scotch Education Department was created, it sat in London as a branch of the English department, where it remained until it was taken over by the Scottish Office, created in 1885. Policy at a crucial stage was thus taken out of Scotland. On the other hand, the priority in 1872 was to provide effective education for all, and the school boards accomplished this by the early 1880s through a massive building and development programme. Unlike England, where a contentious dual system developed in which voluntary church schools greatly outnumbered board schools, the reverse was the case in Scotland where the system consisted almost entirely of board schools: thus, the tradition of national, public provision had been effectively brought up to date in Scotland in a decade. There was no prohibition either on the amount of educational provision that school boards could make beyond the elementary and, slowly, from 1878, a secondary system began to develop in the higher classes in the parish schools, which remained strong in the Highlands and country areas, and in designated schools in the towns. These met the needs of the lower middle classes and skilled artisans to some extent for access to higher education. The ending of school fees in 1889 for the elementary stages and the further siphoning off of local government money to secondary education in 1892 both helped to develop a quite vibrant secondary system which remained relatively open to those who could take advantage of it. There was a serious gap in the provision of some form of further training for the working classes beyond the age of 14, but the inadequacies of the labour market, with its many easy routes for young teenagers into dead-end jobs, were perhaps more to blame here than the school system. The system still remained incomplete in the field of religious education. Since school boards, again unlike England, could teach whatever religious formularies they wished, most of them continued with 'use and wont' – the Bible and the Shorter Catechism – so that the public schools continued to be run on broad Presbyterian lines.[21] This, however, made it difficult for the Episcopalians – and even more so for the Roman Catholics – to surrender control over their schools by transferring them to the school boards. Indeed, the religious provisions of the 1872 Act made it clear that they were not expected to do so. They, therefore, remained outwith the system but were forced to emulate its ever rising standards, undertaking the capital costs of building while relying on SED grants for running costs.[22] Finally, with the development of secondary departments in the schools, the universities could introduce entrance tests, make their curriculums more exacting and suit them, through the institution of honours degrees, to the British career requirements of the Scottish middle classes.

By the 1880s, therefore, in the process of adapting itself to the commercial and social forces transforming British life, the educational system retained many of its traditional features and continued to mark out

Scottish life in significant ways in its adaptation to British norms. Most social classes still used it, even if in specialised sectors, and in country areas the distinctions between secondary and elementary provision were less acute; and a remarkably large number comparatively of the lower middle shopkeeping and upper artisans classes could still find in it a ladder of opportunity either to university or higher status commercial occupations.[23]

Education was also one of the factors which helped to determine the country's cultural and political alignments. In the elections of 1852 and 1857 the combination of Free Church and Voluntary strength which had ousted the old Whigs in the burgh constituencies in 1847 began to break down, partly because of the divisions which the education issue had created between them, while in some rural constituencies, such as Ayrshire, where the Church of Scotland was strong, a candidate's lukewarm commitment to the old parochial system could lose him support. In larger burgh constituencies such as Glasgow, Edinburgh, Paisley and Dundee, this went with a marked move away from the bigotry that had surrounded the anti-Maynooth agitatation, allowing more moderate Liberals to be returned. Such moderates, however, had to take into consideration the new forces which had emerged and, while refusing to allow their actions to be dictated to by any particular religious or social reform interest group, they had to recognise that such interests now existed, and had to be catered for to some extent. Thus, the return of a businessman like Walter Buchanan in Glasgow in 1857, for instance, Whiggish in outlook and cool to franchise reform, was not a reversion to the old governing style. Buchanan had much in common with his working-class constituents in his strong support for the Italian liberals, and he had been a committed Free Trader when his party's leaders still felt such a stance to be impractical. The truth is that in a period of much flux in party politics at the national level, constituency politics depended more on local personalities, territorial support and an ability to promise something to varying interests, none of which was strong enough to dominate, while preventing the Conservatives, the traditional enemies of Reform, from making any sort of a comeback. In short, some moderation and consolidation were the requirements. In such circumstances, the Conservatives became increasingly moribund, being reduced to a mere 15 seats in 1857. As Palmerston's reputation for strength abroad and quiet at home grew, there was a continuous drift to the Liberals in the counties, helped by the increasingly independent attitude of the tenants who, because of the operation of the Game laws and the law of

Hypothec (which gave the landlord preferential security for his rent over his tenant's stock and crop even when these were sold to a third party), began to see their interests as separate from their landlords.[24]

Two trends which became increasingly clear after 1859 were the growing demand for further electoral reform and the growing co-operation between moderate working-class leaders and liberals to achieve this. As the country had increased in wealth and numbers, the anomalies of 1832 had become more glaring. Despite the growing equalisation with England, there were still proportionately fewer Scots qualifed to vote while, at current levels of taxation and population, the total of MPs should have been nearer 80 than 53. The growth of industry in the Clydeside area underlined, in particular, its underrepresentation compared with that still enjoyed by the smaller burghs and rural areas of the north and east. As working and middle-class efforts at co-operation developed, so too did bodies of trade unionists like the Glasgow Trades Council begin to call on trade unionists to play a more active role in politics, to gain greater protection in their working conditions. Their efforts to have the Master and Servant legislation (which penalised servants while protecting masters) amended in 1861 thus led naturally to a joint campaign with middle-class Liberals in establishing the Scottish National Reform League in the autumn of 1866 to press for a further measure of parliamentary reform.[25] The Second Reform Act of 1867 (the corresponding one for Scotland being passed in 1868) – the outcome of parliamentary manoeuvring between Disraeli and Gladstone as each sought their own side's advantage[26] – resulted in the vote now going to householders in the burghs who had been resident for a year and paid the poor rates, and to £5 proprietors and £14 tenants in the counties. This greatly increased the urban vote in Scotland, from 54 000 in 1865 to 154 000 in 1868, bringing many working men on to the registers for the first time. The property qualifications led to a less dramatic increase in the counties, from 50 000 in 1865 to 77 000 in 1868.

However, as in 1832, the Second Reform Act was as significant for what it did not as what it did do. While many working men now could vote in the towns there was no great increase in the number of Scottish MPs that they could hope to influence. Seven additional members were still not enough to reflect the country's importance in either population or wealth. Glasgow and Dundee received one additional member each. Edinburgh was left as before with two, and the creation of a new Hawick district could hardly be regarded as compensating for the joining of Peebles and Selkirk counties. The counties, in fact, came out much better, with Lanarkshire, Ayrshire and Aberdeenshire now divided to receive one extra member each. By limiting urban extensions to existing constituencies and not creating new burgh constituencies for the growing industrial areas in the central belt, Disraeli had kept the counties safe for the Conservatives. The two new university seats simply increased the strength of a professional constituency whose interests were already well represented by the old system. Thus, the anomalies between burgh and country electorates persisted. It was still more difficult to get a vote in the latter. Whereas the proportion of adult men enfranchised in the burghs was now roughly the same as in England, in the counties it was very much lower – about 1 in 24 in Scotland, compared with around 1 in 14 in England. There seemed little reason why a skilled shipwright who was a householder in Glasgow could vote, whereas his fellow worker who lived across the Clyde in Govan in the county of Lanarkshire could not; or why colliers who lived in the village of Blantyre should not vote on the same basis as colliers who lived in the burgh of Hamilton.[27]

In the longer run, however, these drawbacks meant that the demand for more MPs and equalisation between the town and country areas would continue. More immediately, the Act had two related effects. It brought working men directly into the political equation for the first time, raising the question of where their new power would be directed; and greater numbers of voters now meant that constituency politics would have to become more formally organised than had been the case hitherto. Candidates could no longer hope to canvass all of the electorate, and now depended on grassroots organisations such as trade unions, churches and pressure groups to do the organising of the vote for them. Hitherto, Liberal grandees had settled the choice of candidates at meetings in their offices. When the Glasgow Liberals met in the Bath Street offices of the great chemical manufacturer, Charles Tennant, everyone who mattered knew whom to vote for. Town electorates were now anonymous masses. This was particularly the case in Glasgow, where the 'minority' clause allowed the electors only two votes for the three members. To ensure the return of three Liberals there at the general election of 1868, all of whom represented the different interests in the constituency from the moderate to the radical, required organisation and discipline; and the fact that the new working-class voters succeeded in doing so by subordinating their own preferences to the party's interests demonstrated their support for a strategy of alliance with the middle-class Liberals. This is all the more significant in that one of the candidates supported by working men was a textile businessman who had recently expressed his opposition to the minority clause, on the grounds that it might allow interest groups like Roman Catholics or trade unionists to capture a seat! Two-member constituencies such as Edinburgh and Dundee displayed similar support by the new voters.

Such co-operation with middle-class Liberal leadership is not surprising, since the new voters were those who did not flit from house to house and paid their rates regularly. They were thus likely to be from that upper artisan section which shared the same values of self-help – and of co-operation rather than confrontation – as their masters. The number of times the Liberal newspapers congratulated the new voters on their upright behaviour at the polls shows that they were behaving as they hoped they would, faithfully imitating the middle-class. However, this does not mean that they could always be taken for granted. Political action was one strategy out of many by which they saw some possibility of achieving greater gains, and it may have been encouraged by the optimistic atmosphere engendered by the economic expansion of the times. There was a strong minority opinion, however, most effectively articulated by Alexander McDonald and others in the Co-operative tradition, that in the end working men would have to rely on their own political efforts to achieve meaningful change in their lives. The questioning of candidates about such things as housing conditions, which began to be made in the 1870s, suggests that much of the present allegiance to the Liberals was not unconditional and that if expectations should be disappointed then some reassessments might follow. Nor should it be assumed that all working men automatically supported the Liberal party and reform. That nearly a quarter of the Glasgow electorate voted for the Conservative candidate in 1868 indicated that there might be some potential for that party in the new extended electorate, ready to develop if conditions should become favourable. For the moment, however, the Liberals swept all before them in the 1868 general election, winning all of the burgh seats, leaving the Conservatives, still suffering because of their apparent lack of concern for the tenant farmers' interests, with a rump of only seven seats in the counties (see Table 3.1).

After its success in disestablishing the Church of Ireland in 1869 and introducing the ballot in 1872, however, Gladstone's first ministry began to lose favour, because of its failure to concern itself much with the lives of Scottish tenant farmers or working men. In addition, the recent

Table 3.1   Election results.

|      | Liberal | Conservative | Liberal-Unionist |
|------|---------|--------------|------------------|
| 1868 | 53      | 7            | –                |
| 1874 | 40      | 20           | –                |
| 1880 | 53      | 7            | –                |
| 1885 | 62[a]   | 10           | –                |
| 1886 | 43      | 12           | 17               |

[a] Includes four Crofter MPs.

onslaught on the Established Church in Ireland, and the contentious issues of how far religious education should become part of the new board school structure, provided the Conservatives with a religious rallying cry around which to build support. There had already been efforts to put the party on a better organisational footing. A Conservative Association had been formed in Glasgow in 1869, significantly with Orange support, and the opportunity to get candidates favourable to religious teaching on to the new school boards led to further grass-roots support for Conservatism. Elections to the school boards were by the 'cumulative' vote, a system of proportional representation to protect minorities, with each voter having as many votes as there were places. Allocating them all to one or two candidates could ensure the return of a particular interest, and this required organisation. This helped the Irish to build up some political expertise, but it was also used by the Conservatives. The champion of the Bible in the School in Glasgow, Harry Alfred Long, was one such organiser, who regularly topped the school board poll and was also prominent in support of the Conservatives in the west of Scotland. Throughout central Scotland it was in this context that many prominent Conservatives first made their name. In the 1874 election, therefore, the Conservatives staged something of a comeback, winning 20 seats, including three in the burghs. Although much of this was re-occupying ground which they had given up since 1859 rather than fresh gains, it did indicate that large sections of the electorate could be won over by making a more determined effort, particularly in the urban areas of the west, where the growing strength and order in the Roman Catholic community were challenging ultra-Presbyterian confidence. In the counties, the failure of the Liberals to do much for the tenant farmers also played its part. Thus, although many of these seats were to be regained by the Liberals in 1880, a basis had been laid, particularly in western burghs and industrial counties such as Ayrshire, Renfrewshire and Dunbartonshire, on which the Conservatives could challenge with more confidence than had been the case at any time since 1846.[28]

Religious issues played a continuing role in reviving party fortunes along sectarian lines. Irish Church Disestablishment in 1869 had rung alarm bells within the Church of Scotland, forcing some of its leaders, like John Tulloch, to take their first steps into the political arena in order to build up support for their position. Calls to disestablish and disendow the Church of Scotland were raised by the United Presbyterians (UPs) and the Free Church in 1872 and 1874, who started to put pressure on the Liberals to commit themselves to legislate on these lines. The principal reasons for the emergence of this issue stem from the relative strengths of the various denominations and significant alterations in theological and moral outlooks. By 1873, the majority in the Free Church had had their Union negotiations with the UPs, aimed at strengthening their positions, baulked by a mainly Highland minority who wanted to retain the old idea of a National Church. This had the effect of pushing the Free Church further in principle towards the voluntary position which it already occcupied in practice. By the 1870s, both the Free Church and the UPs found themselves in competition with a revived Church of Scotland, now growing at a faster rate than its rivals. A new sense of social mission was running through all three denominations as the older sterner theological outlook changed to an emphasis on the fatherhood of God and the consequent brotherhood of all his children. In competing to reclaim the lapsed urban masses, therefore, the Church of Scotland with its official position and endowments was regarded as having an unfair advantage over the Free Church and the UPs. For all of them, the fact that the Roman Catholics were prospering with the loyal adherence of an urban working-class constituency was a further challenge to their effectiveness. Disraeli felt that he was strengthening the position of the Scottish establishment when he abolished patronage in 1874; but this action, instead of removing the fissures in Scottish public life, merely reinforced them. It was immediately seen as a snare which would tempt the unwary back into the establishment. As the Free Church leader, Robert Rainy, succinctly put it, if a boy had broken a window and then put his hand in to remove the stone, the window was still left fractured: so too with patronage, the stone which had broken the Presbyterian window. The issues raised in the Claim of Right in 1842 regarding the freedom of the Church and the limits of the state were still left unresolved. What the state had just given could as easily be rescinded. Increasingly, therefore, the Voluntaries of the Free and UP churches sought to resolve it by getting the Liberal party to pledge itself nationally and at constituency level to a policy of disestablishment. Since at this time the forces of Voluntary Dissent in England were also mounting a vigorous disestablishment campaign, part of that drive to radical democracy symbolised by Joseph Chamberlain, their hopes of support were high. Gladstone's insistence on proof of widespread support from the constituencies before he would commit himself to Scottish disestablishment made them all the more determined to swing the party to their side.[29]

Little of this seemed to disturb the normal tenor of Liberal ascendancy in Scotland. In 1880, they once again swept the board – 53 Liberals to seven Conservatives – carried along in the fervour of Gladstone's Midlothian campaign, in which he linked his Scottish origins with a new moral view of international relations. Sixty or so local Liberal Associations expressed their adulation in addresses 'honouring him for the breadth of his sympathies with the afflicted and oppressed throughout the world'.[30] However, at the local level the Liberals were in some difficulties. Partly this was due to the fact that having been for so long the only party in Scottish political life, any new issues were bound to affect them more than they would the Conservatives. Their 1874 electoral reverses had persuaded them that they too needed some organisational stiffening. Their carelessness had been most obvious in Glasgow, where a seat had been given away needlessly; various sections in the party, attempting the luxury of running five candidates, had split the Liberal majority between them, allowing a Conservative to slip through. In 1876 and 1877 they had set up an East of Scotland and then a West of Scotland Liberal Association principally to rule on organisational matters, especially on future candidate choices. In 1881, these combined into a Scottish Liberal Association. The representatives of the constituencies, however, sought to influence this new national body to commit it to a radical programme which would be binding on all candidates. For a party containing so many diverse interests, and which saw itself as the national political forum reflecting the needs of landlords, tenant farmers, commercial leaders and working men, such actions were bound to prove divisive. The provisions of the Third Reform Act of 1884–5 further complicated the situation. This finally equalised the vote in the counties and the burghs, leading to a large rise in the total electorate, from 293 000 to 561 000, the greater part composed of Highland crofters and Lowland industrial workers. It thus became a more diverse and less predictable national constituency and less easy for any one party to cater for. More importantly, its redistribution arrangements finally gave Scotland something like a fair share of MPs (72 in all). After abolishing the Haddington and Wigtown Districts of Burghs, seven extra seats were given mainly to the industrial counties (four to Lanarkshire, and one each to Fife, Perthshire and Renfrewshire) and seven to the large cities (four to Glasgow, two to Edinburgh and one to Aberdeen). However, these (with the exception of Dundee) were now arranged in single-member constituencies, so that it was no longer possible to run candidates representing different shades of opinion in harness. Candidate selection thus became an even more vital and divisive factor in local politics, as contending groups on issues such as disestablishment sought to ensure that their man won the nomination.[31]

At the first meeting of the Scottish Liberal Association in 1882, the disestablishers sought to commit the party to their views, but the traditional leaders like Lord Fife sought to temporise as long as possible, arguing that 'the Association was merely one for purposes of organisation, and not for the advancement of any particular political question'. However, the issue had been raised in Parliament by the disestablisher MP for Kilmarnock Burghs, J. D. Peddie, in 1882 and again in 1884, and could no longer be suppressed. The Scottish branch of the Liberation Society (Liberation of Religion from State Control) called for it to be made a test question for choosing candidates at the next election: 'what was needed in Scotland were good men and true as Parliamentary candidates, men like Cromwell's Ironsides who, knowing their duty would fearlessly do it'. In reply, the Church of Scotland set up a Church Interests Committee to co-ordinate a political counter campaign, and Tulloch's remarkable organising skills were shown in his achievement in raising a monster petition against disestablishment, signed by over 500 000 church members together with 150 000 adherents of other churches, in just three weeks in 1885.[32] As Church Defence Associations began to spring up in the constituencies, they 'began to take on something of the complexion of a political meetings'.[33] In constituencies as far apart as Ayr, Inverness, Glasgow and Edinburgh, the Liberals began to find themselves split between rival factions and rival candidates. The Conservatives, on the other hand, as the traditional champions of the Established Church, could only benefit. Already in 1882 Lord Salisbury had advised them during his visit to Scotland to base their efforts at revival on the Church cause.[34] In various constituencies lifelong Liberals, like Edward Caird in Glasgow, were threatening to abstain or vote Conservative as the lesser of two evils if a disestablisher were chosen as the Liberal candidate. At Church defence meetings, church Liberals increasingly began to act in public with Conservatives, fulfilling Rainy's warning to Gladstone that once accustomed to such co-operation they would move out of the party altogether. The final sign of division seemed to be the formation in September 1885 of a National Liberal Federation in Scotland, in imitation of Chamberlain's English body, formally committed to disestablishment and in rivalry to the leadership of the Scottish Liberal Association.[35]

Under pressure from Gladstone and his lieutenant in Scotland, Lord Rosebery, despite numerous double candidatures, unity was maintained in the 1885 election and the Liberals once again won handsomely, with 62 seats to only ten for the Conservatives; a sharp contrast with England, where the Conservatives made large inroads in the borough constituencies. However, below the surface several significant changes had already occurred. Although winning only one burgh seat, Kilmarnock, the Conservative vote had gone up markedly in urban as well as in rural constituencies. Also, they now had, in the Church, an issue on which they could build up their appeal as a 'Scottish' party defending a vital national institution; and, more importantly, they had broken a mould which had existed in many burghs since 1832, by accustoming some Liberals to at least contemplate the possibility of questioning their traditional allegiances. In addition, there were other issues on which they could capitalise. When Gladstone took office with the help of the Irish Nationalists in early 1886, his announcement that he intended to solve the Irish problem by granting a measure of Home Rule seemed, therefore, the final straw to the many whose loyalties had already been shaken in 1885. His gradual shift in this direction had been known to those at the level of high politics for some time, but it came as a bombshell in the constituencies and appeared, along with his recent alliance with Parnell, to indicate simply deviousness and expediency and greed for office. The result was a very large and damaging secession from the Liberal party in Scotland (with a higher proportion of MPs and supporters leaving than in the rest of Britain) and the rapid establishment of a strong Liberal Unionist party by May 1886, ready to act along with the Conservatives as a counterweight to the traditional Liberal predominance in Scotland.[36]

In the 1886 election, 17 Liberal Unionists were returned along with 12 Conservatives as the Liberals fell to 43 (59.7 per cent of the Scottish constituencies), their worst result since 1841. Just as damaging as the loss of seats was their spread across the country, with nine in the west and eight in the east, ranging from Argyll down to Ayrshire plus three in Glasgow, and from Inverness and St Andrews to Roxburgh, Peebles and Selkirk, and one in Edinburgh city. This suggests that Liberal unpopularity was composed of several elements. Part of the loss had already begun with the defection of moderate churchmen in 1885, and the 1886 results merely confirmed the process of disenchantment felt by many at the radical direction the party seemed to be taking. It is significant that many of the leading lights responsible for setting up the new Liberal Unionist Associations in the west and east of the country were those who had been most prominent in seeking Conservative support against the disestablishers in 1885. However, radicals, too, such as A. Cameron Corbett, disestablisher, teetotaler and social reformer in Tradeston, or Charles Fraser-Mackintosh, Crofter MP for Invernessshire, also defected. Some of their opposition sprang from radical dislike of Gladstone's proposals to buy out the Irish landlords with British taxpayers' money. However, like many others, they also objected much more fundamentally to the incipient break-up of the United Kingdom. This did touch a widespread feeling in Scotland, where so much of the credit for the political and material progress of the country was seen as due to the Union with England, especially at a time when Great Britain and its Empire seemed to be becoming ever more isolated by international rivals seeking to weaken it. In the west of the country there were widespread fears that a semi-independent Ireland might seek to protect home industries or, conversely, that economic recession due to Home Rule would lead to another flood of poor Irish coming to compete in the job market. This was a telling argument in the midst of the great economic slump hitting the heavy and associated industries of the west of Scotland in the 1880s. Finally, there were the accusations that their co-religionists in the north of Ireland in particular would suffer from 'Rome' rule. This was sounded not only in the west but also in the east, where prominent UP disestablishers like Dr Calderwood now threw their weight behind the Liberal Unionists. When added to fears that Ireland would become a base from which all 'the dynamitards of Europe' might threaten Britain, the *Dundee Advertiser* felt forced to admit that 'such feelings simply indicate a settled dislike to any recognition of self-government as far as Ireland is concerned'.[37]

Perhaps the basic truth lies in the broadness of that generalisation. Any proposal to give Ireland some measure of self-rule, no matter how limited, raised the whole issue of British and indeed Scottish attitudes not only to Ireland, but to the impact of the Irish in their midst. It is not surprising that the first reaction, therefore, to Gladstone's new move should be bewilderment, and that voters should vote for the man in possession on personal grounds. Nearly all of the 17 Liberal Unionists were already sitting members. Many who wanted to follow Gladstone therefore simply abstained when presented with a Unionist in 1886 as, conversely, did many when presented with a Gladstonian incumbent. The larger issue mirrored one which had also confronted Irish immigrants ever since their arrival in Scotland: how to adjust so as to overcome challenges without at the same time losing their identity. Questions of conflict and assimilation had struck varying responses from the host society too, in which the dominant note had been to welcome evidence of stability in the growth of parishes, schools and occupations and organisation and participation in public life. Under this, however, there had always been widespread suspicion, ranging from the outright hostility shown by the revived Orange movement since the early 1870s to the traditional suspicion and dislike of anything Catholic. The agricultural depression of the later 1870s had increased the flow of immigration to Scotland, renewing fears of job competition. By the 1880s there were over 300 000 Roman Catholics, making for a highly visible social presence, well represented by many new churches and schools. Since the 1860s they had become increasingly active politically, making their weight tell increasingly in the new electoral situation created by the Second and Third Reform Acts, and in the school boards under the forceful leadership of men like John Ferguson. For many, the idea that a group which existed in the poorest areas with the lowest jobs should be regarded as capable of self-rule, and that to a degree not envisaged for Scotland, jarred. In line with current Darwinian and Imperial social nostrums, they would have agreed with Salisbury's judgement that some races were designed by nature to be ruled by others for their own good. For others, there had always been a radical sympathy with the Irish, and the status of local Irish political activists like Ferguson, whose friends included national figures such as Michael Davitt, added to his reputation with progressive thinkers in Scotland. It was through such contacts that Irish accommodations and links with Scottish movements were built up. However, it would inevitably take time for the rank and file Liberals to catch up with the breathtaking leap made by Gladstone. Because the Irish made up a much larger proportion of the Scottish population and impinged on the Scottish psyche more insistently, the Home Rule issue constituted a defining moment in modern Scottish political life so that decisions taken in 1886 determined habits and outlooks which were to last right up to 1914.[38]

Finally, the prolonged downturn in the Scottish economy which began in the 1870s also provided more grounds for the reassessment of Scottish Liberalism which was going on in this period. Because of the prosperity and stability that had been enjoyed since mid-century, this sudden reversal was felt all the more keenly. Changes in the manufacture of steel and the natural rundown of indigenous supplies began to affect the pig iron sector. This in turn reduced demand for coal. Colliers who had been making eight shillings a shift in 1873 suddenly found their wages being reduced, because of declining demand, to around four shillings per shift in 1874. In such an integrated economy, the drying up of orders in the Clyde yards in the 1880s after a period of prolonged output of ships further exacerbated the situation. To cap this, the later 1870s also began to witness the first assaults by the beef and wool producers of America and Australasia on British agriculture. Highland estates, used to high incomes from sheep and sport, suddenly found themselves in a scramble to maintain profitability when wool prices plummeted. Beef prices, too, fell both in the Highlands and in farming areas like the northeast. The marked improvement in incomes and living standards in the crofting and farming areas since mid-century meant that such reversals were as keenly felt there as in the industrial regions. Higher expectations now made groups as disparate as coal miners and farm labourers and crofters unwilling to accept a drop in living standards as an inevitable part of economic laws. The 1880s, therefore, witnessed a revived debate on the whole question of the nature of society and the distribution of wealth in a way which had not been evident since the 1830s and 1840s. In the Highlands this manifested itself in a well-organised Crofters movement. This was partly the culmination of a series of campaigns such as that waged by John Murdoch, the editor of *The Highlander* newspaper (1873–83), to resist any further erosion of Gaelic society. In the Lowlands, similar efforts had been made by cultural enthusiasts like Professor Blackie, or the growing number of Celtic Societies, which contained many radical land reformers who gave voice to the crofters' grievances. Some of it was due, too, to those Social Darwinists who feared that the nation would decline under the ennervating conditions of industrial life unless it was constantly renewed by a strong stock from the country. Much of it was stimulated by Gladstone's other attempt to solve the Irish issue, his Land Act of 1881, which had helped to establish a system of small farming proprietors. Crofters increasingly imitated the agrarian resistance tactics of the Irish, withholding rents and defying the sheriffs, particularly in the district of Braes in Skye in 1882. To defuse the situation, in 1883 the Gladstone government set up a Royal Commission under Lord Napier to investigate the crofters' grievances and, in order to coordinate crofter action for this, a Highland Land Law Reform Association was also set up in 1883. The extension of the vote to the inhabitants of the counties in 1884 thus provided this new body and the crofters with the means to make their revolt effective. Throwing off their traditional deference to their landlords, they put up five Crofter candidates against old-style Liberals in 1885, four of whom won.[39]

In the Lowlands, too, economic fears had a twofold effect. For the Conservatives these provided an issue on which again they could claim to be standing up for vital Scottish interests. Heavy industrial giants such as the Bairds had always been Conservatives, primarily out of religious evangelical conviction, but in the 1870s and 1880s it was becoming clear that heavy industry in general was beginning to move behind that party. Major shipbuilders like John Scott of Greenock and William Pearce of Govan stood as Conservative candidates in the 1880s, the latter successfully in 1885 and 1886, while Sir William Beardmore, the proprietor of the great Parkhead Forge, was a prominent supporter. In the 1885 election, the Fair Trade call gave the Conservatives a strong card to play in heavy industrial areas facing increasing foreign tariffs. Great play was made of Beardmore's decision not to stand in Camlachie, preferring instead to provide its constituents with bread-and-butter employment, while giving the party his general support.[40]

Trade and social conditions also provided material for an electorate which in background inclined to the radical Liberal tradition but was now increasingly ready to listen to ideas which questioned the old economic orthodoxy. Already in the 1860s and 1870s, working men in Glasgow and Edinburgh had begun to raise social issues such as the effects which inner-city clearance schemes might have on their housing conditions. They had already begun to suspect that Improvement Acts promoted by middle-class Liberals might benefit the former more than working men. While the health of city-centre business areas would improve, those cleared from the wynds would begin to press in on nearby artisan housing areas, causing them in turn to deteriorate. Now, the circumstances surrounding commercial failures such as the City of Glasgow Bank in 1878 raised wider, more insistent demands to re-examine the morality of business ethics and, indeed, of the whole commercial culture on which Scottish Liberalism had hitherto flourished. Leaders of opinion such as the Free Churchman, Robert Rainy, and the up-and-coming popular Congregationalist preacher, John Hunter, as well as younger left-wing men, began to call for a re-examination of the casual assumptions behind Free Trade and a rejection of the view that the sole purpose of economic activity was profit. The ideas of land reformers like Henry George therefore received a ready welcome for their analysis of urban social ills. His tour of Scotland in 1884 was a huge success, and a Scottish Land Restoration League was set up in 1884 which ran five candidates in opposition to the offical Liberals at the 1885 general election. Although none of them were successful, their prodding and questioning were forcing radical Liberals more and more to take on board the land issue as well as its urban connotations.[41] Socialist bodies, too, such as the Social Democratic Federation and its off-shoot, William Morris' Socialist League, also proved attractive to many of the younger men. Once again, although limited in their electoral impact, it was their ability to influence the more thoughtful activists which was important in the long run.[42] It was the growing number of younger men like Keir Hardie, Bruce Glasier and James Shaw Maxwell for Labour, and John Ferguson for the Irish, who were to be increasingly important in determining the debate over the future of radicalism in Scotland. Keir Hardie, like the Crofters, represented a new generation which was unwilling to take a passive attitude and now wanted to play a larger role in policy making. For such men, events like the Blantyre pit explosion in 1877, which had killed 207 miners, stiffened their resolve to make owners more responsible for their workers' welfare and to involve the state more directly in caring for their dependents. Increasingly, Hardie began to urge trade unionists into a more aggressive defence of their rights. For the moment they were still willing to ally with the Liberals to achieve this, but Hardie's decision to break away and form an independent party for working men in 1888 had been a possibility that had been in the making for some years.[43]

The general election result of 1885 appeared to confirm the pattern established since 1832, of Scotland as a Liberal country with social values which distinguished it from the rest of the United Kingdom.[44] The creation of a Secretary for Scotland in 1885 seemed final acknowledgement of its distinctive nature. This Act had come about because of growing pressure since the later 1870s both from public opinion and from Scottish MPs, reinforced by the considerable weight that Lord Rosebery could bring to bear on Gladstone. The increasing role of government in public life raised fears about administrative over-centralisation, and the perception that Scotland was given a low priority by government was as great as when it had first been pointed out in 1853.

Popular opinion, in particular, wanted education to be taken out of the control of the Vice-President of the English Education Committee. These feelings culminated in a great public meeting in Edinburgh in January 1884, attended by all shades of political opinion, demanding a separate minister to look after and coordinate Scottish administration. As a result, a Secretary for Scotland Bill was introduced in 1884, in the last months of Gladstone's government, and was finally enacted in August 1885 by the Conservatives under Lord Salisbury, who was favourable to the measure. At first it was felt that this new Scottish Office was rather ineffective. The Scottish Secretary had no seat in the Cabinet and the post was held by a rapid succession of ministers. His main responsibility was for education; his other functions were less well defined. However, the continuing demand by crofters for more land meant further unrest in the Highlands, and this led to the Scottish Secretary having to take over law and order as well as education; and these responsibilities, plus his general oversight of local government, poor relief, public health, roads and so on, meant that he soon became the focus for all Scottish matters. This showed that, as governmental administration developed, its mere existence would inevitably attract more business to it.[45]

This raised interesting possibilities as to how Scotland's identity within the United Kingdom would develop, but the Scottish Office had appeared just at the time when the old world of 1885 was ending and new political directions were appearing. As the Scottish Secretary became a shaper of policy, the desire to monitor his actions also inevitably grew. Since the Scottish MPs had little opportunity for debating Scottish business in parliament, much of the policy of the Scottish Office was developed by the permanent officials and this heightened the feeling that administrative devolution should be accompanied by more political devolution. This was intensified by the fact that, almost as soon as the office was set up, the Conservatives were in power for most of the years between 1886 and 1906, so that the Scottish Office was run by a party which was usually in a minority in Scotland. Up to 1885, support for Scottish Home Rule had run across the parties, but in 1886 the Irish issue polarised Scottish politics and changed the context in which they operated. Irish Home Rule stimulated demands for a Scottish parliament and led to the setting up of a Scottish Home Rule Association in 1886. While the Conservatives were willing to develop the administrative powers of the Scottish Office, after 1886 they were firmly opposed to any political devolution. It is not surprising, therefore, that the Scottish Liberal Association added Home Rule for Scotland to its other radical demands in 1888.[46] By 1886, therefore, much had changed in Scottish life. Its politics were moving in new directions. It had been given a much more formal administrative identity. Running through all this was a new concern about the condition of society and the moral basis that should guide it. At present, much of this was muted, and ideas that general class interests might not always be the same as traditional craft interests were only just beginning to be discussed. The assumptions of former years were now having to give way to questioning in all areas of life, and there was now a sharper edge to the debate which made the future less certain.

# 4

# REALIGNMENTS: 1886–1900

As the divisions between Liberals and Liberal Unionists became permanent after 1886, the whole tone of public life became sharper. Although the latter included a number who had recently been on the radical wing of Liberalism, their 'advanced' notions were kept in check within the Unionist camp by the need to concentrate on opposing the Gladstonians and keeping their new Conservative allies in power. Some of them, in fact, drifted back to the Liberals, encouraged by that party's policy in Scotland of sublimating contentious issues under a general attitude of fidelity to Gladstone. By the later 1880s, the Scottish Liberals had become firmly committed to a number of radical issues which had previously been held back by the presence of the moderates; these included disestablishment, land law reform, Scottish home rule, and by 1891 also an eight-hour day for miners, and further franchise and crofting reform. The economic developments of the time, too, encouraged this polarisation. The Conservatives, increasingly vocal in support of the Empire and British commerce, were able to develop their reputation as defenders of vital local interests as the heavy industries struggled to deal with the uncertainties of international trade. These same economic developments, by raising questions about unemployment, wages and working conditions, forced the Liberals to project themselves as having policies which were more relevant to ordinary people than those being offered by the growing Labour movement. Realising that they were fighting for the support of a narrower constituency, less representative now of the wealth and intellect of the country, they became correspondingly less willing to give way to these new forces on the Left. The admixture of new hope and the lessening of the old certainties can also be seen in the economic, social and intellectual developments of these years.

In the economic sphere, the decline of the iron sector was more than offset by the growth of a strong steel industry. From its origin in 1871, it had been closely connected with the shipbuilding sector, and by 1890 the bulk of Scottish ships were now constructed from the new material. Like the earlier iron industry, steel became a dominant element in Scottish economic life, and by 1900 the Scottish steel firms were producing around 20 per cent of the British output. On this basis, shipbuilding output continued to expand enormously in the 1890s once orders began to pick up again, boosted now by the naval building resulting from the growing economic and imperial rivalry with Germany. In the years before 1914, an incredible one-third of British, and almost a fifth of world, tonnage was coming from Scotland. Coal, too, was turning to overseas markets to compensate for the decline in iron making, and the number of coal miners had expanded enormously, from 47 000 in 1870 to over 100 000 by 1900 and 147 000 by 1914, much of the increase coming in the east of Scotland, particularly in Stirling and Fife.[1] There was a Scotland beyond Clydeside and heavy industry too. The lowland agricultural districts, with their more varied base and longer rotations than in the rest of Britain, had weathered the depression in farming relatively well, taking less land out of profitable production and concentrating on quality produce. All the major urban centres continued to develop. Paisley at last began to recover from the textile depression of the 1840s by developing a range of engineering and manufacturing firms. Aberdeen had added to its varied industrial base by becoming the third largest fishing port in Britain. Overall, the enormous expansion in the economy had produced a large and growing tertiary service sector in transport, building, food and clothing, commerce and the professions.[2] Of the million new jobs created in Scotland by the expansion of the Victorian economy between 1841 and 1911 (more than offsetting the loss of 26 000 jobs in agriculture), the great bulk (41.7 per cent) 'were in the service industries providing the infrastructure of industrialisation'.[3]

It was the influence of heavy industry in the overall pattern, however, that was most apparent. This can be seen in a number of ways. One was the continuing urbanisation and concentration of the population into a relatively small area, making Scotland one of the most congested and skewed societies of the time. In 1900, the four major cities of Glasgow, Edinburgh, Aberdeen and Dundee alone contained one-third of the population, most of it in Glasgow. Looked at in another way, the four counties comprising the heartland of heavy industry – Lanarkshire, Renfrewshire, Dunbartonshire and Ayrshire – contained

44 per cent of all the people living in Scotland, the bulk of them crammed into one- and two-room houses. Other urban/industrial areas such as the Lothians, Fife, Tayside and the north-east, with the exception of Dundee, generally had a more varied economic structure but on a smaller scale. Over-concentration on the great staples of textiles, steel, shipbuilding and heavy engineering was not in itself a bad thing as long as they continued to be profitable, as they were up to 1914. After all, this is what they did best. Nor did it necessarily preclude new areas of growth, as the early appearance of automobile and precision engineering manufacturing ventures in the later 1890s showed.[4] It could be said, however, that it failed to produce a service sector sufficiently large and prosperous in which new ventures could develop, and this generally had an inhibiting effect on the general standard of living throughout the country. Professor Lee's figures demonstrate that growth in service jobs across central Scotland was considerably below the overall British average in the Victorian era, especially in the largest and fastest growing sector of Clydeside. Edinburgh was the only area with the kind of mix resembling that of the Home Counties likely to produce new growth, but since it represented a smaller section of Scottish society its multiplier effect was less. In this sense, heavy industry produced a skewed economy to match its skewed society. Put bluntly, this meant that although wage rates for artisans began to move towards British levels by around 1900, Scottish society in general remained a low-income one with a consequent low demand for services and consumer goods. This ties in with other evidence that in a labour market receiving lower wages and facing relatively higher living costs, there were still glaring gaps between employer and employee, and between the skilled, semi-skilled and unskilled.[5]

On the surface, however, when compared with conditions in mid-century the period between 1870 and 1900 could be seen as one of marked improvement. The general fall in prices meant that for those who remained in work real gains were made. Even allowing for the rapid downturns that could follow equally rapid upswings, affecting groups such as the coal miners or shipyard workers, incomes were better than they had been in the 1850s and 1860s. More significantly, there was now an expectation that there ought to be some sort of minimum standard of living and an increasing rejection of the idea that life should be determined solely by the market forces of supply and demand. In lowland agricultural areas, also, most farm workers found themselves better off at the end of the century than they had been in 1870, not only in terms of income but in housing and diet and general amenities. Here, again there was the paradox of this leading to higher expectations and less satisfaction with rural conditions and working practices, with consequent migration to the cities or overseas. General figures of income and prices mask many variations, but the general impression is one of advance between 1870 and 1900 as prices fell and wages advanced. In the Highlands, too, some of the former pressures on crofters eased, although land hunger and raids on deer forests continued up to the later 1880s. The 1886 Act may not have provided a solid basis for economic growth, but it did give something which had historically been lacking and on which much might be built – security of tenure, compensation for improvements and fair rents. Arthur Balfour's policy as Scottish Secretary in the Conservative government after 1886 was to crack down hard on further crofter unrest by sending police, backed by marines, to the worst affected areas and imposing prison sentences. But it was combined, too, with a policy of constructive Unionism. Government subsidies began to be provided to develop the Highland economy, through help to the fisheries and in the construction of roads and piers. Subsidies to shipping and the extension of the railway to Kyle of Lochalsh by 1897 and to Mallaig by 1901 made communications easier. When they took office again in 1895, the Conservatives began to make some moves towards enlarging holdings through the Congested Districts Board Act of 1897. The region still suffered from deep-seated problems, but they were now being viewed from a quite different perspective in 1900 than that which had led to so much conflict in 1882.[6]

The bulk of people in Lowland Scotland benefited from a gradual decrease in working hours at this time. Railwaymen could still be forced to work shifts of 12 hours and more, and while domestic servants might have security of employment this had to be offset against almost constant calls on their time, apart from the traditional day off. However, in general the working week had fallen from about 60 hours in the 1850s to about 54 by the 1880s. This is reflected in the marked increase in organised leisure, which was one of the most notable feature of this period. All the major towns witnessed a growth in the number of music halls, concerts and choral and musical societies, while with the more general Saturday half-day came a growth in spectator sports of all sorts, from cycling and rambling to cricket and, in particular, association football. When England played Scotland in April 1872 there was an attendance of 4000, and by 1878 this fixture attracted 20 000. By 1890, a

Scottish League was needed to create order amongst the various football clubs and, incidentally, to ensure that they maximised their incomes, while increasing crowds led to the erection of permanent stadiums.[7]

There was a general environmental improvement with the application of the 1892 Burgh Police Act and the establishment of county councils in 1889. The former imposed uniform controls over environmental conditions in towns: the latter reduced the number of units responsible for health from over 1000 to just over 300, making for more rational administration, and obliged the rural areas to appoint medical officers of health. By the 1880s, too, water was beginning to be provided in city tenements along with water closets and this, together with a better diet, may be part of the explanation of the constant lowering of the death rate in this period. Generally, a more watchful eye was kept on public health, not only through the spread of hospitals and the work of the growing band of public health officials, but through the more systematic picture of everyday family conditions revealed by the work of the school boards. Glasgow was vigorously tackling its city problems with a series of policing and health measures aimed at improving the lives of its inhabitants. In 1890 and 1894, it brought electricity and the tramway system under public ownership to add to its earlier provision of water and gas. Other cities such as Edinburgh followed the same pattern. The demolition of the worst tenements in Edinburgh's old city-centre parishes and the opening up of thoroughfares like Chambers Street and Victoria Street led to the lowering of the death rate in these formerly congested areas, although it was still twice as great as that in the more favoured New Town. Similarly, Aberdeen's great drive to coordinate its town planning and improve its provision of services can be dated from the 1880s. The existence of a Scottish Office in 1885 now provided a centre which could take an overview of local conditions, although it was perhaps indicative of its difficulties in getting to grips with modern Scottish life that it could not do much for the first delegation to call on it – Edinburgh Trades Councillors concerned about the effectiveness of the factory inspectorate.[8]

Poor housing conditions, however, continued to be an obstacle to improvements. Despite increasing pressure from reformers and medical experts, too many houses still consisted of one and two rooms, 17.6 and 39.9 per cent respectively by 1901, better in the case of the one-room type since 1881 (26 per cent), but not in that of the two-room (38.9 per cent). The numbers living in three-room houses did grow from 16.4

per cent in 1881 to 19.3 per cent by 1901, but this did not alter the overall situation significantly: 11 per cent still inhabited one-room houses and 39.5 per cent two-room houses compared with 18 per cent and 39.5 per cent in 1881. Overcrowding, therefore, remained high, with 45.7 per cent of the population in 1901 living more than two to a room. The cities, especially Glasgow with its swollen population, contained the greatest problems, but others differed only in scale. Dundee's medical officer blamed its uniformly poor tenement conditions for a quarter of that city's mortality. By 1911, small burghs such as Kilsyth (71.6), Clydebank (69.0), Cowdenbeath (67.6) and Hamilton (65.7) had worse percentages of overcrowding (measured at more than two persons per room) than the large towns such as Glasgow (55.7) and fewer resources to tackle the problem. Even Edinburgh with its sizeable middle class and skilled artisan population, the best of the Scottish cities, had an overcrowding level of 33 per cent, which was no better than the worst English areas.[9] All towns had a common pattern of shared water closets and the problems of congested communal living to contend with. Such conditions marked Scottish society off sharply within Britain, but there were other significant legal and administrative differences. Rentals in Scotland were generally taken yearly and rates were paid by the occupier directly. This meant that working-class families had to budget to take account of possible loss of earnings and opt for the cheapest house compatible with decency. House rents tended to be collected not by owners but by factors who, to make a profit for themselves and the proprietors, had to balance what their tenants could afford against required returns on investment. The result was a constant battle between tenants and factors, with summary ejectment notices running at a very much higher level than in England. Remission of rates because of poverty also prevented many tenants from remaining on the electoral registers. It was small wonder, therefore, that housing conditions should have been such a major issue for trades councils and labour pioneers in Edinburgh and Aberdeen no less than in Glasgow, or that land issues should have played such a large part in creating a working-class consciousness throughout Scotland in these years.[10]

There had been measurable but limited improvements in living conditions, therefore, but many problems inherited from the past were still to be overcome. Despite the remarkable economic growth of the era, it has been estimated that around a quarter or so of the workforce was still casually employed and thus engaged in a constant battle with poverty.[11] Regional variations in wages and prices also make it notoriously difficult to generalise about overall improvements in living standards at this time. This can be seen if the cities with the worst examples of poverty, Glasgow and Dundee, are compared. In the former in 1890, about 27 per cent of the male workforce were earning less than 20 shillings a week on average, the minimum needed to keep a family just on the poverty line. However, Glasgow was a buoyant city overall, with many more opportunities which made it quite distinct from Dundee. The latter was not only a one-product textile town – mainly jute – with few employment alternatives (by 1900, 36 per cent of its total adult population were employed in textile production), but the bulk of this workforce were women, who outnumbered men in the ratio of 2:1. Improvements in wage levels there simply represented a change from desperate poverty to poverty. The average wage for its adult female juteworkers in 1886 was 9s. 7d. which, by 1906, had risen to only 13s. 5d.: the averages for their male counterparts were 19s. 4d. in 1886 and 21s. 7d. in 1906. The resulting social imbalances pushed overall living standards far lower than they ever reached in Glasgow.[12] For the great majority of workers in industrial Scotland in the 70 per cent or so above the ranks of the casual and unemployed, there were other pressures on incomes in this period. New technology and working practices across a range of occupations from bootmaking to riveting were beginning to erode the skills of some traditional craftsmen and expose them, too, to new uncertainties. General economic downturns as in the middle 1880s, or again in 1892–3, 1895, 1903–5 and 1907–10, could mean short time or periods of unemployment for skilled men, in which recent advances were wiped out. The resulting social tensions, the difficulties of labour to organise its numbers effectively, and the failure of Scottish MPs to get their political masters or the new Scottish Secretary to address such issues readily, lay not so much in the ethnic, religious or cultural divisions within Scottish society as in the distortions provided by its particular economic structure. This is a point which will be returned to when examining why such an advanced industrial society should be so slow to produce a strong voice for its workforce.

If there seemed to be a greater spread of material benefits, why should the feeling become much more widespread in this period that there was still much to be done? Perhaps the answer lies in the analysis that the American land reformer Henry George presented, one which had made such a great impact on his Scottish audiences (see Chapter 3). George pointed to the visible and glaring contrast between the opulence of the few and the poverty still experienced by so many: that it was in those societies which had become more advanced where 'widespread destitution was found in the midst of the greatest abundance'.[13] This last point struck home particularly. The perspective of a century or more of technical development had now made people aware that their lives were no more secure and that, like the miners mentioned in the last chapter, wages could plummet in a matter of days. Thus, while the absolute measure of poverty over time might be diminishing, it was increasing relatively as people became more aware of the distances that separated the classes. Thus, the new movements of the time such as the Land Restorationists, the Socialists or the Georgites, with their advocacy of a Single Tax on land, were manifestations of a growing questioning of *laissez-faire* economics. Men were beginning to think that there were other social elements to be taken into account in making up the balance sheet of the nation's wealth.

Such views encouraged an analysis of contemporary social ills and economic strains which pointed not to the personal inadequacies of individuals or their failure to adjust to modern living but to defects in the environment and market in which they had to live. Since these prevented men and women from achieving their full potential, then the state ought to play a more interventionist role in ironing out any imperfections blocking fair competition. It is often imagined that such attitudes, which found their full expression in the New Liberalism developing from the later 1890s, had little foothold in Scotland. While this may be true of its parliamentary representatives before 1906, it is far from being the case at the level of ideas and opinion-making in the general debate going on within the country. One instance of this is the growing concern beginning to be shown by the mainstream churches about the condition of society. From the 1870s, worries about the alienation of the masses despite the ever greater provision of churches had sparked off a series of self-analytical surveys. This growing concern was behind the attack on patronage in 1874, because it was seen as making the church too comfortable, secure and inward-looking. The subsequent calls to challenge themselves and for greater pooling of resources and unity helped to spark off the disestablishment quarrel as to who was the more committed, the Voluntaries or the Establishment. But this increasing investigation into the lives of ordinary people in the effort to understand what prevented so many of them attaining any sort of decency also brought concerned churchmen face to face with the realities of squalid tenement conditions and low incomes. In 1888, the Presbytery of Glasgow began an inquiry into housing which, in its report of 1891, significantly moved beyond a crude analysis based simply on character defects to a recognition that much squalor and poverty was also due to environmental conditions. This signalled an important shift in outlook. The decade saw an increasing amount of literature from churchmen calling for more ameliorative action to be undertaken by public bodies to remove the handicaps from which so many people suffered through no fault of their own. Once the prospects of disestablishment by political means began to fade after the Liberal defeat in 1895, the United Presbyterians and the Free Church, too, began a similar process of reassessment of their relationship with the wider community in their search for a new way forward.[14]

This thinking was also strongly reinforced by the Idealist philosophy being taught at the Scottish universities at this time. As their student numbers increased, new generations were being encouraged to adopt the ideas of civic responsibility being propagated by men like Edward Caird and Henry Jones. Contemporary industrial disputes such as the great coal strike of 1893 made Caird long for a better solution to such economic difficulties than the blind antagonism between capital and labour, and this stress on co-operation rather than conflict was reflected in his teaching and social action.[15] Like Green, Caird believed that the state should be the organic development of all its individual members, and that it should act to ensure the fullest development of all. If there was anything which prevented the right each person had to develop his potential, then the state might intervene to create conditions which would help and not hinder that moral evolution. The moral community of all mankind should be accomplished by mutual help towards that end. The great problem of the day, declared Caird, was '. . . how to raise the estate of man organically . . . [not] . . . to elevate a few at the expense of the rest, but to raise men as a social body in which none can be left behind without injury to all others . . . [with] . . . the greatest effort directed to the class that is most numerous and poor as the class that is most in danger of being left behind. The problem is to level up and make and keep society organic and not to let any class or individual fall out of the ranks.'[16] Caird tried to practise what he preached in initiating a Glasgow University Settlement Association in 1886 which opened a Toynbee Hall in the Townhead district of the city in 1892, as well as helping to found the Women's Provident and Protective League in 1888 (which became the Scottish Council for Women's Trades).[17]

Such ideas found a ready and wide audience in Scotland, because they were putting back into the Adam Smith system of economics the moral basis on which it had been founded in the eighteenth-century synthesis of learning. Such men taught that wealth creation was a social process and not a system of mechanics. It tied in with the views in economics being popularised by Alfred Marshall (whose *Principles of Economics* appeared in 1890), which were also finding much favour with the new professors of political economy, now established in the Scottish universities after the reforms of 1889, such as William Smart in Glasgow or J. S. Nicholson in Edinburgh. Marshall stressed the tentative nature of economic analysis, seeing it not so much as a set of fixed doctrines as unalterable as mathematical formulae, but rather as a means to a body of truth. William Smart, a pupil of Caird, taught in a similar vein. To him, wealth had responsibilities as well as rights: like Caird, he was concerned about social conditions, living standards and the exploitation of women workers: for him, the economist should be concerned about supplying some answers to these issues. Their larger view of the past gave them a greater sense of the complexities of the present. Although they were not collectivists, the steady drip of their ideas on the public mind was directing it in that direction and away from unquestioning belief in the inevitability of market forces. Like Caird, they believed that there were inadequacies in the present system of economic competition and that these should be ironed out by government taking active steps to equalise conditions so as to give everyone a fairer chance in the struggle for existence. Sweat-shop wages which caught women and their families in a poverty trap should be banned. Hours of work should be regulated to allow better domestic conditions to develop.[18]

The miners' agent and journalist James Keir Hardie had the dour determination needed to take such ideas further and put them into practice by organising the political and industrial strength of the workers. His recent experiences in attempting to defend the miners against wage cuts and bad working conditions had led him to the view that state action was necessary to redistribute some of the growing wealth. Since 1885 he had become increasingly disenchanted with the Liberals' ability to deliver this, and was now determined to lead working men in taking political responsibility for their future into their own hands. In 1887, he announced that the miners would begin their own political organisation and in 1888 a by-election in Mid-Lanark gave him the chance to show how sincere the Liberals were about supporting working men's interests by offering himself as the Labour candidate. Despite the largely working-class nature of the constituency, composed mainly of coal miners and iron workers, the local Liberals did not give Hardie a clear run and chose a Welsh barrister, J. W. Philipps, to fight the seat against the Unionist, J. Bousfield. The result was disappointing for Hardie, who came last in the poll with 617 votes, as against 2917 for Bousfield and 3847 for Philipps. It seemed to show that the Liberals still had a secure hold in working-class constituencies in Scotland. However, the situation was more complex. Commentators since have usually ascribed Hardie's failure to the Irish voters' preference for a Home Rule Liberal as against their labour interests. Certainly, there was a sizeable core of about 1300 Irish voters in Mid-Lanark and, despite the support that Hardie had received during his campaign from notable Irish leaders such as John Ferguson and Michael Davitt, it seems that few of them broke away from their traditional Liberal allegiances. However, in a constituency in which local agents put the total mining and working-class vote at around 6000, Hardie's greater problem was that hardly any of his fellow Scots had supported him either.[19] As the figures clearly showed, even if all the Irish had voted for him he would still have come in third; and Hardie was also concerned at the opposition of 'Some of the local miners' agents, Socialists, too mark you,.... Pure spleen',[20] who were opposed to his candidature. In the circumstances it seems harsh to single out the Irish voters for failing to support Hardie when the majority of Scottish colliers in Mid-Lanark appear to have done likewise. Trade union weakness and internal divisions were clearly also serious causes. Efforts to build up strong county unions, culminating in a Scottish Miners' National Federation in 1886, had ended in failure by the end of 1887. It would take much time and persuasion to convince working men that they should break away from the radical tradition of the Liberals who represented the party most likely to be in power.

While the weaknesses of Hardie's new move stemmed to some extent from the ethnic and religious divisions which divided the working class in such constituencies (where, after all, had so many votes in support of the Unionist candidate come from in such an industrial area?), much more was due, as noted earlier, to the nature of the Scottish economy. Despite the large number of miners, Scottish pits were generally small units, and they were highly localised with each county area being virtually autonomous. This led to great difficulties in organising and coordinating joint action, not only within counties but also between eastern and western miners with their different interests. Their culture, too, and working conditions were not such as to encourage the sort of foresight and thrift needed to sustain long-term union growth, and while these traditional drawbacks were now being overcome, it only needed one disastrous strike or sudden reduction in wages to cause all of the organisation that had been so carefully built up to be swept away. Above all, the coal owners had the whip hand. They generally owned the houses and laid down the conditions of work and pay, and trouble-makers could soon be forced out of an area.

This was part of a wider picture of weak working-class organisation in Scotland. Although new unions had begun to appear by the later 1880s among unskilled groups such as the dockers and labourers, they were still underdeveloped in Scotland. Only the large craft unions had much continuity and strength, and they were federal in structure and more inclined to look after their own craft differentials than the interests of the general body of workers. A survey of 1892 found only 147 000 trade union members in Scotland, two-thirds of them in the western heavy industrial region, and this at a time when the total of industrial occupations must have been over a million. By the mid-1890s less than one-third of the Scottish miners were unionised. Much of the rest of Scottish industry was highly localised and, in the absence of large national unions, Trades Councils were still the main focus for trade union activity.[21] Because they were industrially weak they, like Hardie, were inclined to a political strategy. The latter, however, needed the support of a strong trade union base. It was in an attempt to square such circles that Hardie had acted. What is perhaps more surprising, in the light of these circumstances, is not that he came bottom of the poll as that he did so well. In addition to the weaknesses of organised labour noted above, he had to face all the difficulties of any third party trying to break through in what was a two-party, first-past-the-post system. In addition, although working men in such constituencies had gained the vote in 1884, it was still difficult for them to get their names consistently on the electoral role. The residential and poor law qualifications meant that probably only about three out of every five men were ever on the register at any one time, and these proportions worsened the further one went down the wage and social scale. There was also the major problem of convincing working men that they ought to support separate Labour candidates at elections. Much historical confusion has resulted from assuming that working men would necessarily gravitate to Labour. Their refusal to swing behind socialist visionaries at this time, however, was often based on the realistic belief that the values and institutions that they cherished would be best served by voting for either of the two main parties. The struggle for self-respect represented by Irish

Home Rule, the church connections and self-reliance values of temperance groups, could be as important to Irish labourers and Scottish miners and artisans alike, and as achievable within a traditional Liberal or Unionist allegiance as the more secularly based creeds being offered by the socialists as a solution to their material conditions.[22] Although the Liberals might be justified, therefore, in dismissing such challenges to their traditional leadership in Scotland, the small cloud on the horizon represented by Mid-Lanark refused to disappear. The underlying significance of these years is the consistent determination of Hardie and others to maintain the idea of a separate voice which would speak for Labour politically. By August 1888, he along with others had established the first organised Labour party in Britain, the Scottish Labour Party. At a meeting in Glasgow, representatives from the trades unions, particularly the miners, radicals such as R. B. Cunninghame Graham and J. Shaw Maxwell, land reformers such as G. B. Clark and John Murdoch, and Irish nationalists represented by John Ferguson, agreed a programme with Hardie which combined traditional radical measures such as temperance with labour demands such as an eight-hour day and the nationalisation of mining royalties and minerals.[23] As a party, its early electoral efforts were perhaps inevitably negative, its three candidates polling poorly in the 1892 election, while organisationally it tended to be restricted to the west. However, in 1892, on the initiative of the Aberdeen Trades Council, a United Trades Council Labour Party was formed, which also ran four candidates at the general election. This showed that there were growing linkages between organised labour and those favouring a political strategy.

These new trends were affected by the strong regional forces in Scottish life. The Trades Councils in Glasgow, and in Edinburgh and Aberdeen especially, remained suspicious of the personalities behind the Scottish Labour Party and tended to develop on their own. Aberdeen, although having a more varied economic base, had felt the effects of the downturn of the mid-1880s, its tradesmen having to face competition from other areas and undercutting from the cheap labour coming into the city in search of work. As a result, its Trades Council had begun to encourage the unionisation of the unskilled, and had moved away from its traditional political allegiance to the Liberals to advocating a more independent labour strategy by the 1890s. It tended to choose candidates to suit local circumstances and these did reasonably well, particularly in by-elections such as that in 1896 in Aberdeen North, where Tom Mann, as the sole challenger to the Liberals, won 46 per cent of the vote.

Dundee, too, witnessed a growing Labour challenge, although the starker and narrower one-industry environment left less room for manoeuvre between the strong Irish group, the millworkers and the trades council. Nevertheless, an ILP candidate with local roots did well there in 1895, especially in comparison with Labour candidates in the west of Scotland. In Edinburgh, too, where skilled artisans were beginning to feel that their interests were less secure due to technical changes, a similar shift in outlook can be detected, as new unions of dockers, labourers and tramway workers began to be encouraged by the crafts who ran the Trades Council.[24] By the end of the 1890s, union membership had grown, and with it a feeling that the interests of both the skilled and unskilled now lay more in joint action.

The main achievement of Hardie's Scottish Labour Party was to remain in existence, hoping eventually to profit from these underlying trends in what was still a hostile environment, in which most working men still saw their aims as being fulfilled within the Liberal party. Important groups such as the Fife miners remained firmly Lib.–Lab. and committed to Gladstone. Radical working men of the older generation regarded independent Labour candidatures, as they had the Land Restorationists in 1885, as nothing less than attempts to wreck the Liberal party. When the Independent Labour Party was set up in 1893 in Bradford, following much the same lines as Hardie had in 1888, it at least found an existing base in Scotland with some experience already behind it in the shape of the Scottish Labour Party. Thus, when the latter amalgamated with the ILP in 1894, Hardie's ideas of separate working-class representation were beginning to take root in Scottish political life.

At the general election of 1892, the Liberals regained some of their old confidence in their ability to govern. They were more tightly knit than they had been in 1886. In 1887 and 1888, Gladstone had consolidated his position among his Scottish radical allies who supported him on Ireland by agreeing that disestablishment should be the next great issue to be settled. In addition, the party declared its support for Scottish Home Rule, and since the Scottish Home Rule Association generally consisted of radicals, this meant that they had the main groups behind them. Irish and Scottish Home rulers worked enthusiastically alongside each other for the return of Liberal candidates. The church issue proved to be as prominent and divisive a topic as Ireland at the hustings, and the pressure from the disestablishers became more intense, provoking a corresponding surge of support from the Established church. The Conservative administration's lack-lustre record and its rough handling of Irish and Crofter unrest, however, gave the Liberals a target to aim at.[25] The result was that the Liberals regained ground, winning 50 seats and reducing the Conservatives and Liberal Unionist to 11 each (see Table 4.1). This did not mean a return to the old situation, however, because the Unionists held on sufficiently to con-

*Table 4.1    Election results.*

|      | Liberal | Conservative | Liberal-Unionist |
|------|---------|--------------|------------------|
| 1892 | 50      | 11           | 11               |
| 1895 | 39      | 19           | 14               |
| 1900 | 34      | 21           | 17               |

solidate some of the advances that they had made into urban Scotland in 1886, performing well in Glasgow and Edinburgh (where they retained three and one seats respectively), and in Ayrshire and Refrewshire. The Liberal Unionist and Conservative combined share of the total vote in 1892 (44.4 per cent) was only marginally down from 1886 (46.4 per cent) and it was now at a much higher level than the Conservative share of 1885 (34.3 per cent).

Since Gladstone's priority was to get his second Irish Home Rule bill through Parliament, traditional radical demands and the new social challenges were relegated to second place. When, therefore, that bill was killed off by the Lords in 1894 and Gladstone retired, he left behind him a party which was discouraged by failure, lacking in new approaches and seriously riven by rival groups contending for the leadership. It was clear that the party that had dominated Scottish life for so long was at a crossroads. Party leaders needed the commitment of the activists in the local associations to maintain their positions. The local activists needed to be inspired by the vision of their leaders. The latter, however, became increasingly introspective in this period of transition, affected by the same forces which were moving society. Commitment to the old individualistic values of faddist Liberalism, such as thrift, temperance, economy and disestablishment, had to be balanced with an awareness of the new social questions emerging as to wages, working and housing conditions. In fact, despite the apparent total absorption with Ireland, the 1892–5 Liberal administration had demonstrated some concern over social and industrial issues, such as the long hours worked by railwaymen, and acknowledged that the state had a greater role to play in ensuring industrial harmony.[26] It had also replaced the

Board of Supervision with a Local Government Board and popularly elected Parish councils to ensure more direct government control of public health issues.[27] However, decisions as to which direction to take on such issues were still being considered when the 1895 election occurred, leaving the Liberals on the defensive. The unity hitherto provided by issues such as disestablishment or Ireland was lacking this time. The former began to move out of the political sphere as church leaders began to explore other strategies, while the failure of the Liberals to secure Irish Home Rule, plus the continuing divisions caused by the Parnell divorce meant, too, that the Scoto-Irish began to ponder their traditional allegiances to that party. The failure to have anything to show for their three years in office left the radicals in disarray. The result was a big fall in the Liberal seats to 39 (their lowest share of the Scottish constituencies since the 1830s), as against 33 for the Unionists (19 for the Conservatives and 14 for the Liberal Unionists). Labour performed poorly, too, with an average vote in the eight consituencies it contested of only seven per cent, lower even than Keir Hardie's share at Mid-Lanark.[28] Only a long slogging propaganda and organisational effort backed up by some solid trade union support would improve their chances at the parliamentary level.

Just as the context of the times weakened the Liberals, so it further strengthened the Conservatives. These were years of steady economic activity, during which British industry nevertheless felt itself coming under greater threat from abroad. The strong Imperial policy advocated by Conservatives appealed both to businessmen and working men in Scotland. Maintaining British markets overseas was presented as guaranteeing busy shipyards and workshops at home. Keeping the peace at home and abroad was essential and the Conservatives showed that they could deliver where the Liberals, in 1892–5, had only talked. Constructive Unionism in government aid for the Highlands and Ireland dampened down unrest, particularly in the latter, and reduced pressure for Irish Home Rule, for which few Scottish working men had any enthusiasm anyway. As the Unionists grew more confident, so did the Liberals become more divided. Partly this was due to internal squabbles over who should lead the party and in which direction. By 1898, Rosebery had moved to the sidelines, from where he and followers like Asquith and Haldane could snipe at his apparently weak successor as Liberal leader, Sir Henry Campbell-Bannerman, the MP for Stirling Burghs. The Roseberyites wanted to move the party away from its traditional platform of disestablishment, temperance and Irish

Home Rule, which they regarded as outmoded (and in any case disliked) and, instead, follow a policy of Imperial development and internal national renewal through state-led social efficiency measures. Campbell-Bannerman wanted to follow a more middle course, remaining true to traditional causes while accepting the need to construct new social policies. However, such a course required time to develop, untrammelled by the complications of personal rivalries and ambitions. Much of the national debate had a particular resonance within Scotland. Its leading protagonists came from there. The Scottish press with its wide popular readership gave extensive coverage to the arguments which each side put forward. The rival analyses were viewed in highly localised terms as to their relevance for the heavy industries and businesses of the west with their Imperial interests, as opposed to the more traditional small burgh radicalism of the east and north of Scotland. In this drifting state, the Scottish Liberals became ever more divided, fighting each other rather than their political opponents. Inevitably their constituency and national organisations became more ineffective and their supporters more disheartened.[29]

These shifts in outlook can be detected at all levels from the official to the grass roots in the later 1890s. At the top, the Scottish Office and the Boards that it controlled began, slowly but significantly, to pay more attention to the seemingly intractable problems of unemployment, poverty and social deprivation. Successive Scottish Secretaries, Conservative as well as Liberal, with their officials began to see that the traditional policies of deterrence and coercion did not suit every case and that welfare needs had to be more directly addressed to personal circumstances. Although the Scottish Poor Law still theoretically excluded the able-bodied, an increasing amount of investigation, both official and voluntary, began to suggest a more interventionist approach to ensure better health standards. As noted above, the creation of a Scottish Local Government Board, more directly under the Scottish Secretary's political control, signalled a new and wider outlook, as did the appointment in 1898 of the country's most eminent public health practitioner, Dr J. B. Russell of Glasgow, to the Board as its chief medical officer of health. Similarly, the Public Health Act of 1897 tightened up the framework laid down by the previous 1867 measure considerably, and gave local authorities new standards to aim at, as well as helping to disentangle health from poor law considerations of economy. Although solutions to the basic problems had not yet emerged nationally, at least the questions were now being formulated in a realistic way. It was no longer considered enough now to tell men in the middle of a trade depression that they must find work to support themselves and their families. The distinctions between the respectable and the undeserving no longer seemed so clear cut.[30]

Much of this new thinking stemmed from the continuing concern being shown at the local community level on how to solve the social puzzles thrown up in an industrial urban economy. Caird's influence was continued by Sir Henry Jones, his successor as Professor of Moral Philosophy at Glasgow in 1894, while David G. Ritchie (1893), followed by Bernard Bosanquet (1903), at St Andrews, and Andrew Seth in Edinburgh (1891), were equally important in propagating the same message among their students.[31] Their rejection of individualism and a search for a wholeness of approach in understanding social aims had a widespread appeal in Scotland because it was, in a sense, a reformulation for modern times of the generalist approach of the Enlightenment thinkers of the eighteenth century. Social Unions in Edinburgh and Glasgow were influenced by such ideas, as were ministers such as the young David Watson, a student of Caird, whose experiences in a poor city parish forced him to face the question of how to apply his religion to the social problems he witnessed every day, and led him eventually to found the Scottish Christian Social Union in 1901. The Church of Scotland, both in its own committees and in a series of national Church Congresses which it began to organise in 1899, increasingly advised its members to consider the effectiveness of the church in relation to the social and economic issues of the day.[32] John Hunter, in Trinity Congregational Church in Glasgow's west end, was another important influence in spreading the Social Gospel. His course of sermons in 1899 on 'The Church and the City, the ideal of Civic Life and Duty' was widely regarded as having 'struck a blow against individualism and the business is business attitude to morality and industrial welfare which often goes with it', influencing, among others, progressive civic leaders such as D. M. Stevenson. Hunter sided with Keir Hardie in his attack on Lord Overtoun, one of the leading Scottish evangelicals, in which Hardie contrasted Overtoun's strict sabbatarian attitudes with his chrome works which operated every day of the week and where low-paid labourers worked in appalling conditions.[33] Although given with some qualifications, such open support would have been much less likely ten or twenty years before and was a sign of how far the balance of public opinion had shifted. Thereafter, evangelical sabbatarianism appeared increasingly outmoded and failed to carry much weight politically.

Hunter, like Caird and Professor George Adam Smith of Aberdeen, was a strong advocate of women's rights and supporter of the Scottish Council for Women's Trades, founded in 1895, to protect women and children against the evils of sweated labour. He was also, like Caird, a strong opponent of the Boer War. The later 1890s also saw municipalities begin to move beyond the provision of services which could be justified as necessary for all, like water or gas, and into the building of houses for specific groups such as working men. Although such intervention in the social mechanism was still very tentative and the amount of house building undertaken in the Scottish towns was minimal, it did signal a new determination to adopt a more collectivist approach to city problems. Glasgow was the most advanced in this respect, under such committed exponents of municipal socialism as Sir Samuel Chisholm. Once again, this involved intense argument on which categories should be helped: Was the slum dwellers's necessity due to personal inadequacy and vice, or to simple inability to afford better; and, who was to classify who was deserving and undeserving? Such debates further highlighted the need to analyse what was causing poverty among plenty.[34]

Those trying to advance the interests of Labour argued that poverty was due to inadequate wages and working conditions. Despite their failure to make much impact at parliamentary elections, their analysis proved more effective at the local level. From 1889 and 1890, the first trickle of 'labour' town councillors began to appear in Glasgow, Dundee and Aberdeen. Although their success was spasmodic, it was the result of a more determined effort by the local trade unions and socialists to combine, especially in returning candidates to parish councils and school boards. By 1899, a Workers Municipal Committee had been established in Edinburgh to run candidates in local elections. Before this, a more successful and solid union of local trade unions, the trades council, co-operators, the Irish National League, the ILP and socialists had emerged in Glasgow in 1896 as the Workers' Municipal Election Committee, to ensure that Labour issues such as the eight-hour day, better working conditions and minimum wages for Corporation employees should be supported by Labour representatives.[35] In spite of difficulties, therefore, the challenge from Labour was sustained and the strategy which eventually created the modern British Labour Party, of returning parliamentary candidates backed by trade unions, was thus already being developed in Scotland. Only by asserting their presence politically could the trades hope to have their interests heeded.

A significant boost to this strategy came, ironically, from the exclusion of the more politically active and leftward leaning trades councils from the TUC in 1895 by trade union moderates who had been increasingly irritated by the political criticism levelled at them by these groups. This, however, left the trades councils free to push the trade unions in a leftward direction within their own country, which they proceeeded to do by setting up a Scottish Trades Union Council in 1897. Once again, as in the political and administrative sphere, one of the arguments made to justify the move was that Scottish industrial conditions were often different from those in England and that this, plus geographical considerations, often made English policies unsuitable for Scotland.[36] This further reinforced the Left towards the Home Rule stance adopted by Hardie, in its belief that Scottish society was readier for more radical and collectivist policies. The failure of the prolonged national engineering strike of 1897 was another factor in persuading skilled men that the key to progress lay in political power combined with industrial strength. One can see, therefore, why a Scottish Workers Electoral Committee, combining trade unions and co-operators with the ILP and socialists, should emerge in 1899 before the Labour Representation Committee was set up in England in 1900. In some senses it was an admission that industrial reform could not be gained by union strength alone, but it was also part of a development which can be traced back to 1887 at least of trying to give Labour interests their own separate political voice in Scotland so as to have a say in the forming of their country. From 1886, the constitutional nature of the kingdom was being re-examined; so, too, was the cultural context in which working-class leaders had once been content to accept guidance within the general Liberal tradition.

The same process of shifting to and fro between old and new allegiances also affected the large Irish section among the Scottish working class, making their support for the Liberals less certain. Far from being a tool simply for others to wield, the Irish groups in Scotland had always contained elements who resented too much dictation from above. Both in 1885 and in constituencies such as Glasgow Camlachie in the 1892 election, there was evidence of some Irish support for local Land Restoration and Labour representatives. The constant and, at times, increasingly shrill admonition of the main Irish newpaper in Scotland to keep to the strict party line in voting Liberal suggests that it was not always confident of unquestioning obedience from its readers.[37] The central part played by men like John Ferguson and Michael Davitt, who had strong links with the nascent Labour movement and with radical land reformers such as John Murdoch, also suggests that Irish Home Rule embodied more than constitutional change. The sort of historical self-image which Ferguson was producing from his publishing business, and which Davitt spoke of in his many visits to Scotland, was one in which the future was viewed in terms of common people of all sorts of backgrounds making their own decisions locally, free from the Imperial pretensions of Westminster. It paralleled John Murdoch's appeal to the Gaels' social and economic experiences as justification for their present political claims.[38] It has been claimed that such rethinking failed to influence the Irish in towns such as Dundee, but it did surface in the more complex industrial and social contexts of the west of Scotland. When the failure of the second Home Rule Bill began to loosen old allegiances to the Liberals, an increasing number of Irish there were becoming unionised and taking an active part in local trade union activity. In addition to the Workers' Municipal Election Committee of 1896, the Irish were part of a Glasgow Trades Council joint committee which, along with co-operators and the ILP, worked for the return of mutually agreed candidates to the parish councils.[39] Links were thus being created with those who were trying to get a voice for Labour in local situations – this a decade before the switch of Irish to Labour is supposed to have begun with the formation of John Wheatley's Catholic Socialist Society in 1906. What seems significant in this process is that such contacts were already under way, not because they were directed from above but because they emerged from that group's living and working experiences. At the parliamentary level, political allegiances could thus swing behind the candidate representing the most realistic hope of getting support for Home Rule, and yet at the same time be combined with support for Labour representation at the level at which it affected wages and conditions. This dichotomy can be clearly seen in the 1900 general election, when Irish backing for Liberal candidates was generally withheld because of the latter's support not only for secular education but also for an aggressive Imperial policy. At the same time, they stood alongside Keir Hardie and G. B. Clark at pro-Boer meetings and worked alongside the ILP and trades council in support of the anti-war candidate in Glasgow Camlachie. In the North-East Lanarkshire by-election of 1901, their weight was flung behind Robert Smillie, the Labour candidate, rather than the Liberal Imperialist and anti-Irish Liberal Alfred Harmsworth. While that might be regarded as voting against an anti-Home Ruler rather than voting for Labour, there is evidence in the next by-election in this mining constituency, in 1904, that when an acceptable Liberal stood, much of the Irish vote remained with Labour.[40]

Some of this independence and new outlook came from the more secure social and institutional religious framework the Irish had created for themselves by this time. In the 1890s there were 338 000 Roman Catholics in Scotland, the bulk of them of Irish extraction and located in the west, with sizeable concentrations in Dundee, central Scotland and Edinburgh. They had 244 churches and over 180 schools around which their social and political interests centred. In addition to religious societies, they had a solid welfare system in operation, as well as representatives on local school boards and parish councils. While much of this may have been inward-looking, it did contain elements that ran counter to the current orthodoxies by which the present was linked to the past. In the Catholic press, in education societies and social events the picture of history which was presented went back to a medieval and Counter-Reformation European past, beyond the Glorious Revolution of the Whigs. Like other out-groups such as Labour, or nationalists like the writer Charles Waddie, whose *Why Scotland Lost her Parliament* appeared in 1892, they, too, were discovering where they had come from. Their press also provided them with social comment, giving much space to Leo XIII's encyclical *Rerum Novarum* of 1891, which expressed the Vatican's first cautious questioning of modern economic competition and its concern for the welfare of the worker. Irish immigrants and their descendants reading it would realise that in the communities they had created in their response to industrialism and urbanisation, they had already anticipated much of its spirit. The 1890s were thus a seed time, and not a fallow interval between the end of Victorian values and the beginning of modern welfarism. Far from being a monolithic community blindly supporting a single issue, the Irish – as much as other groups – were reflecting the dynamism and fluidity of the age. Since they lived in the vital middle of that society, it would have been surprising had they reacted otherwise: hence their developing responses in their own way, just as with other sections of the population, to social movements as represented by Labour and national preoccupations as represented by Liberalism.[41]

In the reassessments being undertaken as to future directions, the immediate political initiative inevitably went, however, to those who were most sure of their destiny, and in the years leading up to 1900 that position was occupied by the Unionists. In the aftermath of the Fashoda crisis of 1898, Britain seemed increasingly isolated and her Imperial interests safe only in the hands of Lord Salisbury's Conservative administration. Scotland, and particularly its heavy industrial belt, with its many commercial links and its general concern for the maintenance of British trade, had a close interest in what went on in Africa. The outbreak of war with the Boers in 1899 therefore caused a national closing of ranks in support of the government and the British troops in South Africa. For the Liberals it meant further difficulties. Rosebery and his supporters, like Asquith, Haldane and Munro Ferguson, defended the government's actions, and increasingly distanced themselves from the Campbell-Bannerman wing and the old-style Liberalism they asssociated it with. Campbell-Bannerman and the radicals were less zealous and became increasingly critical of the current mood of Imperialism as the war dragged on, denouncing it in the Gladstonian tradition as the immoral military bullying of small peoples. A substantial number of pro-Boer MPs began to try to counter the current war fever with a series of anti-war meetings in early 1900, but these only served to show that the party was increasingly out of touch with public opinion and internally divided. Starting in Glasgow and continuing in Edinburgh, Dundee and Aberdeen, supported by the ILP, the Irish nationalists and Liberal radicals, such gatherings were smashed up by jingoistic crowds. In Glasgow, a German lecturer in Queen Margaret College, who was accused of writing anti-British articles for the German press, felt impelled to resign. Some Clyde shipwrights marched to demonstrate their support for the war.[42] The relief of Mafeking in the spring of 1900 seemed to show that the forebodings of the old Liberalism personified by Campbell-Bannerman had been proved false by events, and in the September of that year the government capitalised on the current mood by calling an election. Inevitably, the Liberals fared badly. Although they received slightly more votes overall than their opponents, it is indicative of their low morale that they gave the Conservatives a walkover in three seats. The resignation of the Scottish whip, Munro Ferguson, from the Scottish Liberal Association just before polling hardly helped, while the presence of a number of Liberal Imperialists within that body meant that much of its electoral effort was wasted in internal feuding.[43] In the circumstances, it was not surprising that party activists failed to come out to support the party at the polls. The result was a body blow. For the first time since 1832 the Liberals were in a minority in Scotland, winning only 34 seats as against 38 for the Unionists. The latter did particularly well in the west of Scotland where they reduced their opponents to a small rump of six MPs and made a clean sweep of all seven Glasgow seats.

The once mighty Liberal tradition appeared broken in 1900. The shifts in direction which began in 1886 seemed to show that the political culture which had been built up since 1832 was now out of date. Liberals had failed to respond to the times, and the traditional slogans of peace, retrenchment and reform had no appeal either to those who wanted more emphasis on social policies or to those attracted by the Imperial vision. The latter feeling had been mightily reinforced by the part played by Scottish volunteers and the valiant record of the Scottish regiments in South Africa. This fusion of Scottish pride within a British sense of identity made Liberal particularism and squabbling seem parochial and petty. However, mainstream Liberal opinion in Scotland had always been wary of extremes. Increasingly, the jingoists began to overreach themselves, and newspapers such as the *Dundee Advertiser* asked why reasoned debate should be drowned out by mobs bawling the National Anthem. As the expectation that the war would come to an early conclusion waned and its costs continued to soar, the moral courage of Campbell-Bannerman in questioning the tactics involved in waging a war against a guerilla force began to cause a reaction. In 1900, a ginger group of pro-Boer young Liberals formed the Young Scots Society – Home Rule in outlook and dedicated to the study of Liberal principles, social analysis and progressive politics – who threw their weight behind Campbell-Bannerman.[44] Their emergence showed there were still those who believed that Liberalism could be as relevant for the twentieth century as it had been for the nineteenth.

# 5

# NEW DIRECTIONS?: 1900–14

In 1900 the Liberals were in disarray and the Unionists triumphant. Yet by 1906 the position had been dramatically reversed and the latter reduced to a small rump, a pattern which persisted right up to 1914 (see Table 5.1). How had this come about? To what extent did it represent a significant change in political direction? At first the Liberals still seemed to be internally divided by wrangles over future policy.

*Table 5.1    Election results.*

|          | Liberal | Conservative | Liberal-Unionist | Labour |
|----------|---------|--------------|------------------|--------|
| 1906     | 58      | 7            | 5                | 2      |
| 1910[a]  | 59      | 8            | 3                | 2      |
| 1910[b]  | 58      | 7            | 4                | 3      |

[a]January; [b]December.

Rosebery wanted a 'clean slate', free from the old 'faddist' commitments such as disestablishment, temperance and Ireland. He tried to steer the Liberals further in the direction of national efficiency and Imperialism with the founding of the Liberal League in early 1902. This new venture, which was largely Scottish based, only ever took strong root, however, in the west of Scotland, where the Liberal Imperialists' opposition to Irish Home Rule and support for international commerce struck a responsive chord. In Edinburgh and the traditional burgh constituencies, it was more difficult to find support, especially when the war officially ended in May.[1] The lessening of tension and the realisation of the human and material cost of the conflict then induced a swing back to the older faiths, and a distaste for courses which seemed

107

to bring with them the threat of further internal discord. By the end of 1902 and the start of 1903, therefore, mainstream Liberalism, headed by Campbell-Bannerman and supported by groups such as the Young Scots who were determined to get the party back into good shape, was regaining confidence. There was a revival of hope in the new century, a move away from the introspection and uncertainty which had marked the end of the nineteenth century. Events and environment were no longer regarded as being somehow beyond the control of statesmen or people.

Liberal recovery from the reverses of 1900 was further helped by Chamberlain's attempt in 1903 to win over the Conservatives, and the country, to a programme of Tariff Reform. His proposals to replace the existing economic strategy of international competition with one giving preference to Imperial products and protection for British industry behind tariff walls inevitably united the Liberals in support of Free Trade. More seriously for the Unionists, it had a particularly devastating effect on party morale in Scotland. As has been seen earlier, historically there had always been a strong Peelite element among the Scottish Conservatives. Influential organs like the *Glasgow Herald* reflected the commercial attitudes of the west of Scotland in its antipathy to Gladstonianism, but it combined this with a traditional commitment to Free Trade. Despite some support, industrialists and large businesses in the west of Scotland were generally opposed to Chamberlain's new direction. The Liberal Unionists, who had made up such a large part of Conservativism's revived strength in Scotland, were not ready to betray a tradition of which they regarded themselves as the true guardians. The Scottish Secretary, Lord Balfour of Burleigh, left the government because of his opposition to Chamberlain over the issue. In the economic slowdown after the war there was a severe depression in 1904–5, accompanied by disturbingly high levels of unemployment, which did little to make Chamberlain's new crusade more popular. The prospect of dear food in return for job security was not only unappealing in the arena of everyday life; its rejection of Free Trade hit at a theory of economic and social progress that had been a deeply ingrained part of Scottish life since the eighteenth century. By 1905, therefore, it was the Conservatives who now found themselves in deep disarray, while the Liberals were enthused by having a strong, emotional issue around which the differing sections could rally.[2]

In addition, while the Conservatives in England were facing further opposition from Nonconformists because of the benefits which their

1902 Education Act had given to Anglican schools, ecclesiastical developments in Scotland were once again creating a more favourable context for traditional Liberalism. In 1900, the Free Church and the United Presbyterians had negotiated a union (the United Free Church; the UFs) to strengthen their position. The minority of 'Wee Frees', mainly located in the Highlands, who had opposed this union because it signalled a move away from the establishment principle of 1843, claimed all the assets, buildings and so on, as the true descendants of the founding fathers of the Free Church, and won their case in the House of Lords in 1905. In the upshot, to effect a settlement the government intervened to make a proportional distribution of the property. The effect of this was to make the UFs and the Church of Scotland more ready to consider a greater union. If Parliament could interfere in 'voluntary' churches as if they were simply like other corporate bodies, then there was a need for some solution that would guarantee them both national religion and religious freedom. By 1906, the Church of Scotland was offering to explore avenues along which it and the UFs might act jointly. This more co-operative atmosphere was reinforced by the continuing concern as to the Presbyterian churches' social relevance and their failure to maintain a strong working-class membership. In 1904, the Church of Scotland established a powerful Social Work Committee, and by 1910 the UFs had formally opened their Committee on Social Problems. Clearly, there were strong forces at work here, forcing the various churches to grapple with real problems via co-operation rather than confrontation.[3] By the mid-1900s, therefore, those ecclesiastical factors which had formerly weakened the Liberals and strengthened the Conservatives in defending conflicting church interests had now been replaced by a new mood more favourable to the Liberals. At the very least, it allowed the natural bias of a Presbyterian culture towards the party of progress and moral concern to assert itself.

There was a growing mood throughout the country, too, that the Liberals under Campbell-Bannerman represented fairness and morality. Scottish military valour, and Scottish missionary and administrative achievements in bringing learning and good government to Africa and India, were the qualities that made them proud of Empire. However, an Imperialism which smacked only of military conquest and oppression was distasteful. An important element here in damaging the government's reputation was the importation of Chinese labour to work the South African mines. The trade unions were not alone in seeing cheap labour as no less objectionable abroad than at home. It undercut the Scottish worker who hoped to emigrate, particularly to South Africa. It seemed part of a wider attitude in which the interests of British business were put above the food prices paid by its workers. Such arguments contributed to a widespread feeling across the classes that Chamberlain and the Conservatives stood for the rich against the poor.[4]

The Conservatives and their Liberal Unionist allies suffered a heavy defeat in the 1906 election. Some of this was the natural reaction against the party in power. Just as support for the government during the war had been so violent so, too, was the reaction once the conflict had ended. The cost of the war was cited as a reason for the failure to follow social policies at home. It also had the misfortune to be hit by the trade depression of 1904–5. The government received little credit for having acted positively to do something to tackle unemployment with the Unemployed Workmen's Act of 1905. This allowed local authorities to provide temporary work for unemployed men rather than leave them to the legal rigidities of the Poor Law (based on theories of self-help which had been imposed by doctrinaire whig-liberals). However, financial restraints limited their effectiveness. What was remembered, perhaps unfairly, was that Balfour's government had seemed to be able to act more decisively whenever financial interests were threatened. Overall, the landslide appeared to be even more crushing in Scotland than in England: here the Liberals won 58 seats and Labour won its first two seats in Glasgow and Dundee, while the Unionists were reduced to just 12. It seemed as if the natural political order in Scottish political life had been restored after more than a quarter-century of confusion and drift.

The other reason for Liberal success was that Campbell-Bannerman's party was able to fight the election with all sections united in defence of Free Trade, with freedom for the various interests to stress traditional issues such as land reform, social improvement, temperance, and support for the principle of Irish Home Rule. Free Trade could be presented, in what was almost a re-run of the Anti-Corn Law League campaign, as bringing all things to all men – cheap food, cheap manufacturing costs, something which was morally right and part of a universal law binding nations in peaceful commerce. Chamberlain's arguments were too sophisticated to reduce to easy slogans, and many influential business and political leaders distrusted them. Prominent Liberal Unionists such as Alex Cross and Cameron Corbett in Glasgow Camlachie and Tradeston bolted the party line and stood as Unionist Free Traders. Campbell-Bannerman, too, had always been committed to the Gladstonian line on Ireland and, with a promise of devolution as a first step to a wider settlement, gained most of the Scoto- Irish vote. This was enough to satisfy its supporters without alienating the sceptics within the Liberal ranks. In addition, there was a general commitment by Liberal candidates to Home Rule for Scotland, too, so that issues on which its society had a particular interest, such as temperance or land reform, might be dealt with more speedily and effectively. Although there was a growing recognition that the squalor and poverty in large parts of urban Scotland required government intervention and subsidy, there was also strong support for the notion that reducing the effects of alcoholism should be part of that rehabilitation process. More land for crofters and the creation of lowland smallholdings were other issues which had a traditional appeal as necessary extensions of the 1886 and 1897 Highland legislation.[5]

It would be a mistake, however, to see the 1906 Liberal victory in Scotland as simply the final flourish of the old radicalism, containing little promise of the new progressive social policies on which to build for the future. The atmosphere throughout the campaign at election meetings and in the press reports gives a firm impression that they were determined to do something about protecting labour and improving social conditions, particularly housing in rural and urban areas, if they were returned to office. Land reform was presented not only as an attack on landlordism, but also as something which, by reducing migration from the countryside to the towns, would ease pressure on the labour market. Far from being old- fashioned and traditional, Scottish Liberals in 1905–6 felt confident in their claim that they spoke for the broad mass of the population. Unlike England, where an electoral arrangement had been fashioned with Labour not to spoil each other's chances in winnable seats, the Scottish Liberals felt confident enough to contest Labour's claim to represent the people. Labour's relatively poor performance in Scotland (winning just over 26 per cent of the vote in the nine constituencies that they contested) showed that the Liberals were justified in so doing, and it could be said that the two seats which Labour did win were due more to the general Liberal swing than anything else. In Glasgow Blackfriars, Labour benefited because the Liberal candidate, Provand, was regarded as being so little different from the Unionist in his views on Ireland and social policy that the Irish vote switched happily to Barnes, secretary of the Engineers' Union. In Dundee, Irish and Labour support combined to return Wilkie of the Shipwrights' Union in tandem with the Liberal in this two-member seat. Labour candidates failed to make the impact which they had in England, where they had won in 27 of the 45 seats that they fought, coming third in constituencies such as Govan, Glasgow Camlachie, and North-East Lanark, where they had high hopes and where there is evidence they were gaining increased Irish support. On the whole, working-class men seemed to have voted tactically and not on class or ideological lines, supporting the party that had the best prospect of winning and delivering promises of social improvement. The highest morale and greatest activity in party workers was shown on the Liberal side, particularly in the efforts of the Young Scots group during the campaign.[6]

Liberal belief in the relevance of their policies for the future also comes over in the tone of their campaign speeches in Scotland in 1906. There was a new emphasis on the rights of labour and on the need for government to act more positively in order to redress the social balance, especially in towns. There were calls for land reform and the taxation of land values as a means of lessening the burden on industry and creating employment. Campbell-Bannerman's speeches in Scotland concentrated on traditional Liberal items, but they were couched in language that emphasised their relevance for contemporary social concerns. In Stirling, he spoke of Home Rule as a way of speeding up social legislation and giving decision-making back to ordinary people. Upholding Free Trade, he claimed, was not a negative concept but an essential step in helping the poorer classes. He was in favour of the eight-hour day for miners and the need to reverse the recent Taff Vale decision, which had made trade unions liable for damages. James Caldwell in Mid-Lanark proposed that a Liberal goverment should bring in a bill to prevent the eviction of miners from tied houses during trade disputes.[7] In addition, a number of new, progressive young MPs, anxious for a more active social interventionist policy by government, began to represent Scottish constituencies in 1906 – McKinnon Wood, a follower of T. H. Green, in Glasgow St Rollox, and J. A. M. Macdonald, a founding member of the New Liberal 'Rainbow Circle', in Falkirk Burghs. Some of the most prominent advocates of municipal socialism, such as D. M. Stevenson in Glasgow and J. H. Whitehouse in Dunfermline, were important pillars of Liberalism at a local level, receiving valuable reinforcement with Cameron Corbett's return to the Liberal fold. Although still a minority, MPs with advanced social views had become more prominent in Scottish Liberal circles since 1900, like George McCrae of Edinburgh East, whose programme stressed not only temperance, but the need for working-class housing and old age pensions. It was pressure from such MPs which had extended the provisions of the Unemployed Workmen's Act of 1905 to cover Scotland: 'a drastic alteration in the philosophy of Scottish welfare: [because] the unemployed now had a right to public assistance'.[8] Dr Hutchison's detailed study of this period has shown that these years created an atmosphere in which New Liberal attitudes found an increasingly warm welcome in Scotland. The election of J. D. White and P. A. Molteno, followed by Arthur Ponsonby and Winston Churchill in 1908, brought in men keen to develop social interventionist policies which would encourage the broad mass of working people to continue to adhere to the Liberals. He has shown convincingly, too, that in terms of party organisation, finance and grass-roots support, it was the Liberals who registered the most vigorous growth throughout this period. Far from being pressurised by the challenge of Labour, it was the Liberals instead who, by 1905–6, had created the general air of reformism which drew Labour along in its wake.[9]

There were plenty of social challenges for politicians to face in the first decade of the twentieth century in Scotland. The economy still appeared to be buoyant, although this was accompanied by a greater feeling of pressure throughout society, both in trying to remain competitive and to retain security of employment and advances in living standards. Development of the steam turbine and the move to larger down-river yards kept shipbuilding at a high level right up to the Great War, as did the growing naval rivalry with Germany. There was an equally dizzying rise in coal output, as the number of miners climbed to 147 000. The spread of retail outlets, the greater mobility afforded by suburban transport systems and the growth of the big, city-centre shops all suggested a continuing dynamism. However, there were some ominous cracks in the edifice. The most productive pits lay in the east away from the heavy industries. Expansion at such levels was bound to cause painful readjustments if demand should fluctuate or decline. It was becoming more difficult for industrialists to compete in overseas markets for the disposal of products which could never be consumed by the home market. Much of the wealth that had been made from a century of growth had been being invested abroad (from an estimated £60 million in 1870 to £500 million in 1914) in developing new lands. Their products, such as cattle and grain, needed bales and transport and thus tied the Scottish economy ever more firmly to the old lines as suppliers of jute sacking and bulk carriers. There had been a spread of new motor car manufacturing ventures, some of them noted for their technical advances, such as the Mo-Car syndicate of 1896, or the more ambitious and forward-looking Argyll Company of 1906, but they were having to fight their way in a more difficult environment. The sharp recession of 1904–5 was followed by an even deeper one in 1908–10, in which not only the casual workers, but an unusually high proportion of skilled men, now found themselves ensnared. While wages improved during this decade, prices surged ahead, too, pressing down on people's real incomes. The years before 1914 saw the largest ever waves of emigration to affect the country. In the decade 1900–10, it was estimated that the country had lost 254 000 people, greater than the previous mass exodus of 217 000 in the 1880s. This was a sign partly of the desire to maintain the higher standard of living that was now expected, but partly, too, of inability to find a satisfactory life within Scotland. A high proportion of those leaving were skilled families from the central belt, or strong and healthy farm workers from the north. The chief whip, Alexander Murray, the Master of Elibank, notified Asquith with some alarm that whereas there had been nearly twice as many Irish emigrants (19 027) as Scottish (11 495) in 1899, the position had been reversed by 1910, with the Scots (23 136) outstripping the Irish (22 878) for the first time.[10] While the market worked admirably to bring the best return on investment, it did not function as a mechanism for the best social distribution.

Some of that was becoming increasingly apparent through the growing number of investigations into the health and housing of the nation, such as the Royal Commission on Physical Training (Scotland) of 1902–3 (given added urgency by the recent South African war), or local inquiries such as the Glasgow Municipal Commission on Housing in 1902–4, Dundee's Social Union Report of 1905, and the official surveys of Aberdeen, Edinburgh and Glasgow schoolchildren undertaken between 1903 and 1907. The message from these was that, despite the overall improvements in health and environmental conditions, those who lived in the most insanitary inner-city areas had the higher death rates and incidence of disease. Children in areas such as Canongate in Edinburgh or Blackfriars in Glasgow were markedly smaller and slighter than those in middle-class districts like Brunstfield or Hillhead.[11] While eugenicists used such evidence as proof of race decline (as well as reinforcing the political argument that resources spent on welfare were futile), the medical experts more realistically noted how it demonstrated the defects of diet and environment experienced by so many, which could be overcome by more positive help. Their views were supported by environmental studies such as those of the young Dr A. S. Macgregor of the Public Health Department in Glasgow, who showed that after a prolonged spell in Belvidere fever hospital, slum children had improved markedly in height, weight and overall physique.[12] There was a more continuous effort to tackle such issues, especially when the Scottish Office came under the vigorous direction of Sir Archibald Sinclair in 1906 and with his appointment of Dr W. L. MacKenzie as Medical Member of the Local Government Board. MacKenzie was a determined man, who increasingly recognised that improvement would always be hampered by poor housing, and under him there was a sustained drive to achieve at least minimum standards of cleanliness throughout the country.[13]

How much still had to be achieved was made clear by the 1911 Census, which provided much ammunition for those advocating greater government involvement in social policy. This showed that while there had been a reduction in the total of one-room houses and the numbers inhabiting them, there were still great numbers in two-room houses (at 39.5 per cent, the same as it had been a decade earlier), although there had been a welcome continuing increase in the percentage inhabiting three-room houses (to 21.1 per cent, compared with 19.3 per cent in 1901). Many of these homes were still overcrowded: 56 per cent of the one-roomed, 42 per cent of the two- roomed and 24 per cent of the three-roomed. Such congestion was acknowledged to be as bad in rural areas such as the Hebrides or burghs such as Ayr, the only difference being that the deprivation was less immediately obvious there than in the slum areas of Glasgow, Dundee or Greenock. The Master of Elibank wrote to Asquith in 1910 about the need to do something about 'the horrible conditions in the Long Island, especially Lewis, worse than the slums of Edinburgh or Glasgow'.[14] Since shared water closets were the norm in so many tenement properties, it is not surprising that there was a constant struggle to maintain decent sanitary conditions. Insanitary areas could not be knocked down without building some replacements for the dispossessed. With the downturn in building after 1903 it was clear, however, that the market could not readily meet the situation. Builders could not get a return on their money from a population which, in general, could not afford the type of houses needed for better physical and moral health. There were still too many small burghs lacking the resources or the expertise to provide a lead locally and respond adequately. Experts in the Scottish Office or in the more progressive municipalities were beginning to realise that some public action was necessary which would necessitate higher national spending. At least there now seemed to be a better understanding of the situation and of the need for a more coordinated response.[15] Part of this was the greater concern shown for the welfare of women and children. The 1908 Children's Education Act, as well as providing compulsory medical inspection, had empowered school boards to feed and clothe necessitious children. There was growing awareness of the need to support mothers in their efforts to improve their homes, especially in the encouragement of better cookery and dietary arrangements.[16] Much local philanthropic effort went into fresh-air holiday excursions and the provision of play areas for children. The work of bodies such as the Scottish Council on Women's Trades and local surveys strengthened the movement to get better protection and working conditions for women, who tended to be overrepresented in the lower-paid occupations throughout the country. This was belated recognition of the crucial role which women had played in the emergence of a successful industrial, urban Scotland. Although they had remained in the background during much of the country's changing history, this does not mean that they were passive endurers of change. Ever since the first alterations had begun in the countryside in the mid-eighteenth century, they had been directly involved in all the great forces that had shaped the country's history. In much of Scottish agriculture, or in manufacturing sectors such as textiles, their labour had been vital. In these they had learned skills of organisation and had gone on strike to assert their rights.[17] Such decency and morality as had been achieved in Scottish life over the century was due largely to their constant efforts to maintain cleanliness and family coherence and inculcate virtue in the midst of overwhelming difficulty. Many of the world-betterment and philanthropic organisations at a local level had been made possible only through their continuous background support. In Anti-Slavery or Chartist groups they had played a prominent part, particularly in the former which, through the work of Quaker women such as Jane Smeal in Glasgow and Eliza Wigham in Edinburgh, had followed the Garrisonian line of direct feminine participation. Much of the voluntary, charitable work of the century and the institutional growth in school teaching, orphanages and hospitals would have been impossible but for the devoted labours of so many women. Roman Catholic nuns played a crucial role in the development of stable communities among Irish immigrants. There seems, too, to have been a culture in

Scotland that encouraged women to play a rational role in society. It had always been expected that the public provision of education would include girls as well as boys. At the higher levels, from the 1860s there was an increasing demand coming from the ranks of the professional classes for a greater political voice for women. In the 1890s the movement for women's higher education had won its main battle in Scotland's ancient universities, before those of England. When the direct pressure of suffragists began in Scotland in 1906, it thus took on the gradualist and rational characteristics of the movement that had already developed north of the border. Within the constraints of Victorian and Scottish male attitudes to women, they played a role in Scottish society which was far from passive, a complex mixture of earner, money manager, defender of individual and family rights (as in the Clearances, or in the many industrial disputes initiated by women workers from the 1830s onwards, or sustaining families during men's strikes, or in conflicts with house factors) and, above all, as survivor. This groundswell of concern for women was another factor directing public attention to issues such as low wages, poverty and environmental congestion.[18]

In other ways, too, the age exhibited characteristics which belied its low environmental standards. It was in this period that cities and towns began to develop greater visual interest and variety, with the growth of town halls, theatres and public buildings based on architectural forms that blended Scottish and European traditions eclectically and confidently. The lighting of town centres with their great store window displays made them a centre of attraction for artisans and their families, who found in them some of the light and colour missing in their everyday lives. It was an age of new, more intellectually aware developments in the visual arts and literature, a style which can be seen percolating through to influence the illustrations and content of the popular Scottish press. Most of the art galleries, public halls, great parks, libraries and theatres which marked Scottish life for much of the twentieth century had their origins in this pre-1914 period. King's theatres were opened in Glasgow (1904), Edinburgh (1906) and Dundee (1909); Aberdeen had His Majesty's (1906) and Ayr The Gaiety (1902), while many other burghs had their music halls. In all, the number of theatres in Scotland grew rapidly, from 32 in 1900 to 53 in 1910 (15 of which were in Glasgow). This was the age that saw the flowering of the Scottish pantomime tradition, as well as the first attempt to present drama as an art form and intellectual challenge, with the formation of the Glasgow

Repertory Company (influenced by the Abbey Theatre movement in Dublin) in 1909.[19] Musical life in Scotland could also be said to have seen its first major development in this period with the consolidation of the Scottish Orchestra Company and the Edinburgh and Glasgow Choral Unions, and the formation of the Glasgow Orpheus Choir in 1906. When Edinburgh's magnificent Usher Hall was opened in 1914 it was perhaps typical that the programme should have included an Imperial March by Elgar and a selection of traditional Scottish airs. Despite a century or more at the forefront of British industrial advance, Scottish society still retained strong traces of sentimentality. Such cross-currents reflected the general ambiguity before 1914 as to the links between high and low culture, new and old nostrums, upper- and working-class relationships and future political directions.[20]

In its early years, the 1906 Liberal government maintained the momentum derived from its massive electoral victory. The threat to trade union funds posed by the Taff Vale decision of 1901, for instance, which had made these bodies liable to be sued for the actions of their officials, was removed by a Trades Disputes Act of 1906. In 1908, a system of old age pensions was introduced, which was deeply popular among ordinary working people. By 1908, however, the worsening recession was causing difficulties, which were reflected in the loss of a number of by-elections to the opposition. The government was rescued from this by the intransigence of the Lords. Lloyd George proposed a Budget in 1909 which would provide both increased naval output to counter the German challenge, along with a commitment to future social expenditure (such as sickness and unemployment insurance) through new income and land taxes on the rich (including one on the unearned increment of land). Foolishly, and against constitutional practice, the Lords rejected the budget, allowing the Liberals to regain the initiative by calling an election in January 1910 on the popular cry of the Peers versus the People. In this the Liberals managed to maintain their lead over the Unionists but only very narrowly by 275 to 273 seats, and now depended on the support of Labour and the Irish Nationalists. This bald summary is necessary to put the Scottish trend into perspective. Here there was no similar swing of the pendulum back to the Unionists and against the party in power. Instead, the Liberals beat all comers, winning 59 seats to only 11 for the Unionists, with Labour retaining the two that they had won in 1906. Some observers dismissed this simply as reflecting the innate conservatism of Scottish Liberalism based on loyalty to the Gladstonian tradition and an inbred attachment to the old individualistic radicalism of temperance, anti-landlordism and Smilesian self-help.[21] However, there is much evidence to suggest that such an analysis is superficial and that the 1910 results, far from being due to the inward-looking nature of a 'Celtic fringe', untouched by movements of thought which were currently agitating the rest of Britain, were solidly based on a widespread popular belief in the continuing political relevance of the Liberals as a party in tune with the way in which society was developing.

The strength in depth of the Liberals electorally in 1910 showed that the 1906 result was no temporary flash in the pan based on the somewhat unusual circumstances created by Chamberlain's Tariff Reform campaign. When a second election was held in December to force a limitation of the blocking powers of the Lords, the results were almost the same (58 Liberals and 11 Unionists) with the exception that Labour took the largely mining constituency of West Fife, to bring their total up to three. Liberal strength was widespread throughout the country, and they ran strongly, too, in the few seats that the Conservatives did win, pressing them hard, for instance, in Ayr Burghs. The extent of their recovery from the trough of 1895–1900 is convincingly illustrated if their performance in 1892 (taken as representing their peak year in the late-Gladstonian era of realignment) is compared with that of January 1910 (taken as representative of their pre-1914 position and when their win of 1906 had begun to lose some of its shine). In 1892 they took 53.9 per cent of the votes cast as against 44.4 per cent for their Unionist opponents: in 1910 they still retained 54.2 per cent of the popular vote as against 39.6 per cent for the Unionists and 5.1 per cent for Labour. In terms of votes cast, they had increased their total by 97 903 (an increase of 38.1 per cent) since 1892, compared with an increase of 50 089 for the Unionists (23.8 per cent) since 1892, against a total increase in turnout of 185 312 (39 per cent) over this period. Furthermore, in the 12 by-elections they fought between 1906 and 1910 they retained all their seats, contrary to the national trend. Given that Scottish society was experiencing the same social and economic trends as the rest of Britain, and that discussion on contemporary social issues or on international affairs was as vibrant here as elsewhere, there is a prima facie case to be made from the electoral results alone that Scottish society still thought that the Liberals were relevant.[22] In addition, they faced little threat from voters switching their allegiances readily to Labour. Labour's three seats by December 1910 contrasted poorly with the 38 that their counterparts held in England. Labour contested 11 seats in Scotland in

January 1910 and had come third in nine of these, with only 20 per cent of the popular vote. In December 1910, Labour contested only five constituencies. Willie Adamson, the miner who captured West Fife as their third Scottish seat, was from the old Lib.–Lab. mould rather than from those on the Labour Left, intent on supplanting the Liberals. A fiery left winger, J. O'Connor Kessack, won 29 per cent of the vote in Glasgow Camlachie to dish the Liberal, but elsewhere in the industrial belt only Robert Smillie performed reasonably with 26 per cent in Mid-Lanark, where the voters preferred to return a well-known social radical in J. W. Whitehouse. Although there is evidence of Irish voters transferring to Labour, the re-emergence of Irish Home Rule as a possibility, with the Nationalists now holding the balance of power in the Commons after 1910, obviously conditioned their tactical voting.[23] These figures suggest that, despite the growing number of trade unionists in Scotland and the affiliation of the miners to the Labour party in 1909, voting for the Liberals was just as much a preferred option for Scottish working men who hoped to achieve better social and working conditions. It is no surprise to find miners from Fife arguing at the Scottish Liberal Association conference in Dunfermline in October 1910 in favour of the Osborne judgement, which had freed them from having to pay a political levy to Labour 'for the spread of Socialist doctrines of which they altogether disapproved'.[24]

Liberal policies also could still blend traditional interests with contemporary social concern. Temperance was an old-fashioned issue, but its stress on personal reform was still seen as one of the necessary paths to social transformation which, along with environmental improvement, commanded strong support from influential elements in the working class, both Catholic and Protestant. The Scottish Prohibition Party which was founded in Dundee in 1901 was as much a Labour as a temperance party and its founder, Edwin Scrymgeour, helped oust Winston Churchill there in 1922, standing as the Prohibition and Labour candidate.[25] More significant was the question of land reform. This, too, could seem out of date in its anti-landlordism but, as the recent Peers versus the People election campaign had just shown, it was still a powerful rallying cry for all those opposed to privilege and dedicated to achieving greater social equality and fairness. It had a particular resonance in Scotland, where important proposals to extend the provisions of the Crofters' legislation to all tenants under £50 and create more smallholders, as well as proposals for land valuation with a view to further taxation, had been thrown out by the Lords in 1907 and again in 1908. These proposals would have given greater compulsory powers to create smallholdings than was the case in England and there was no doubt that the Scottish Secretary, Sir John Sinclair, intended to use them vigorously as a means of reducing current levels of unemployment. After 1910 there was increasing pressure from within Scottish Liberal ranks for further extensions of land legislation in the form of taxation of land values. Lloyd George's movements in this direction in his 1909 Budget and in his Land Enquiry of 1912 were widely welcomed in Scotland, especially by the increasing number of Scottish MPs who wanted greater direct government action to tackle the country's legacy of social ills. Once again, these land proposals were presented as a form of redistributive taxation. Shifting the burden of taxation from industrialists and businesses on to the unearned increment enjoyed by those who benefited from mere ownership would stimulate the economy and provide employment; as well as making more money available for social reforms, by reducing land costs it would make it easier to build houses and solve a major Scottish social problem. The Land Act, finally passed in 1911, along with the new National Insurance provisions, thus allowed the Scottish Liberals to present themselves as broad enough to cater for both traditionalists and innovators in the party, while at the same time holding themselves out to the electorate as having more realistic and attainable policies for social welfare than Labour.[26]

This is not to say that there were no signs of dissatisfaction with existing political ideologies before 1914; only that they did not seem to be capable of being turned into widespread support for alternatives based on class. There was, for instance, not only an increase in trade union numbers but also greater willingness by their members to act more aggressively in defence of their interests. The union membership of miners, which had been 57 000 in 1900, grew to 78 000 in 1908 and 86 000 by 1910. There had also been marked growth among traditionally weak groups such as dockers and transport workers and the semi-skilled and these were often led by socialists or ILPers. A well-led Scottish Farm Servants Union was established in 1913. The years before the war witnessed not only the violent conflicts of the dockers in 1911, the miners in 1912 and transport workers in 1913, but a rash of strikes ranging from the Singer Sewing Machine works at Clydebank and Pullars dyeworks at Perth to skilled engineering shops. Despite their syndicalist connections, these outbreaks were mainly to defend wages and conditions against rises in the cost of living and the growing tendency of employers to cut costs by shedding labour. Although many of these employers represented the same economic outlook as the Liberal and Unionist parties and, indeed, were often their prominent supporters, most workers seemed to view such conflicts as part of the normal struggle to maintain working practices rather than as steps in the crusade to bring about a socialist commonwealth.[27]

Nor were socialist alternatives to the prevailing economic and social nostrums lacking in liveliness in Scotland at this time. The decade before 1914 saw a rapid increase in ILP branches, and the establishment of the socialist newspaper *Forward* in 1906 under the editorship of Tom Johnston gave them wide publicity. John Wheatley had founded a Catholic Socialist Society in 1906 in an effort to direct Scoto-Irish political muscle towards social reform. In ideas, novelty and general sparkle, the Left in Scotland had much going for it at this time.[28] In addition, in housing it had a central issue that might determine the politics of the future. Some of the features which made housing an issue so peculiar to Scotland as compared with England have already been touched on: the multi-occupancy, often by different types of tenants, within the same tenement block; long lets inducing caution in renting; overcrowding and lack of facilities with their constant threat to domestic decency; the confrontational relationships between tenants, especially wives, and house factors over rents and conditions and the constant struggle to maintain 'respectability'. It was an issue which was bound up with all the current arguments over redistributive taxation, incomes, a living wage, the causes of poverty and 'slumdom'. It was a condition which was widespread in rural as well as in urban Scotland and which united trade unionists and Labour politicians in the separate cities and towns and regions in a common programme – to get rid of the blots and build replacements through public funding. At a time when local rates were generally rising sharply anyway to pay for better services, the idea of subsidising part of the community by ratepaying professional and business classes, shopkeepers and better-off artisans was one on which a class-based ideology could be developed. The way in which the rent issue quickly polarised political interests along class lines in 1915 in Scotland, causing a revulsion against the small-business governing class who were the backbone of Scottish Liberalism, proves this.[29]

However, Labour's poor record in the few by-elections that it contested between 1910 and 1914 showed that it failed to capitalise on such undercurrents of discontent. This may have been due to its poor electoral organisation. ILP activity and liveliness was not accompanied by great growth in Labour party membership. There were divisions between trades councils and the few constituency Labour parties as to who should lead. Finance was always a problem. The Co-operative movement stood aloof. Efforts at greater party organisation were only being undertaken with some sense of purpose in the major cities such as Glasgow, Edinburgh, Dundee and Aberdeen, as late as 1912–13.[30] The Liberals could also still outflank Labour on the housing question. Many of them were beginning to advocate greater public intervention to tackle housing deficiencies. Their 1911 House Letting Act answered a long-standing working-class complaint by reducing the length of lets. In 1912 the Liberal Scottish Secretary set in train a wide-ranging Royal Commission to inquire into housing conditions, in response to pressure from the miners. As his officials began to collect evidence, their shock at what they found stiffened their resolve to achieve wholesale change.[31] A larger electorate which included all men and women might have produced a different set of electoral priorities and changed the political climate. However, this will never be known, because before it happened the war intervened to change the whole situation radically. All the indications are that it was the Liberals who were gradually adjusting more successfully to the social and economic trends of the time than their Labour rivals. As long as the old progressive ideologies held sway and the majority of people felt that they could hope to prosper within the system through co-operation rather than class war, the dice would always be loaded in favour of the status quo. Only a fundamental, widespread change in outlook, coupled with a sharper sense of unfairness between the classes, might change this.

In any case, Labour critics of the traditional parties, seeking to replace the economic system which these parties represented with a new vision, often seemed more intent on alienating working men than weaning them from their traditional allegiances to the Liberals or Conservatives. ILPers and socialists were never slow to scourge 'the feckless', 'loafers' and 'drunkards', or decry the general propensity of working men to put the immediate satisfaction of their wants before the long-term self-denial and sacrifice needed to create a socialist commonwealth. There was a coercive element in the future they offered which taught that men and women would have to be conditioned into the habits needed to sustain the new utopia. Socialist housing reformers were just as keen as the most rigorous poor law officials on disciplining the dwellers in the 'farmed out' houses in the slums into better habits.[32] It is not surprising, therefore, that the bulk of the population, at every level of labouring, skilled and semi-skilled, should make different choices as occasion demanded: trade union for some working protection; benefit/co-operative society for sickness and funeral expenses; church group, lodge or sporting club for social support; and Liberal or Conservative for political choice as the most realistic hope of altruistic treatment from those who governed them. The Scoto-Irish, overwhelmingly working class, were the most coherent and identifiable example of such a variety of attitudes coexisting beside each other. Their participation in trade unions was growing, a trend encouraged by offical church teaching. Some wanted to combine this with a more active support for labour politics, but at the municipal rather than the national level. Home Rule as presented by men like Michael Davitt carried a promise of greater power to people like them and perhaps some escape from the poverty which constantly dogged them. Membership of the United Irish League also provided a degree of support for their social and employment concerns, which was often more effective than any currently provided by trade unions. Its associated benefit societies insured them against sickness and unemployment. In addition to their faith, a host of parochial organisations provided meaning, status and opportunities for culture and colour in their lives.[33] If skilled Scottish working men were cautious in their response to Labour and satisfied with their commitment to traditional party politics, why should the great masses below them, made up of elements like these Irish immigrants and their descendants, have acted any differently?

Liberal Scotland thus showed a remarkable capacity to adapt to all the changes that it had experienced during a century or more of growth and transformation. This is, perhaps, most obviously shown in support for the idea of some form of home rule for Scotland which had been achieved in the years before 1914. Scottish Whigs had spent the early years of the nineteenth century in dismantling the feudal, aristocratic institutions of the past as barriers to progress. Their Liberal successors then spent much of the later period in reconstructing institutions in ways which would allow them to retain control of the processes by which they might flourish more readily within an expanding Britain. The creation of a Scottish Office had been the result of the need to provide some general oversight of the increasing role of government in Scotland. From the outset it had taken over not only control of education, but of most of the Home Office functions for law and order and general superintendence of local government, police, health, inspection of mines and so on. To this had been added the Crofting legislation for the Highlands, a new stronger Local Government Board in place of the old Board of Supervision, a Board of Agriculture as a result of the 1911 Land Act, plus a separate Board of Commissioners to administer the National Insurance provisions of 1911. Its increasing expertise and willingness to intervene in health and welfare questions, and the way in which a strong-minded holder of the office could utilise its powers to implement more active, interventionist policies, was widely recognised. Increasingly, therefore, as it grew in power the MPs began to demand some account of its administrators' actions. During the 1890s and 1900s a series of home rule resolutions and then bills began to appear, with those of 1912 and 1913 receiving a second reading and the support of the majority of the Scottish MPs. Part of their argument was the practical one that it would ease parliamentary congestion at Westminster. But there was also the more radical idea that it would allow for legislation which was suited to Scottish aspirations and institutions. The Liberals were the main but not the only supporters of home rule. Scottish Labour leaders had held such views from the beginning, seeing it as a means of transforming society and, despite the official anti-devolution line of the Unionist leadership, there was a great deal of grass-roots sympathy on that side, too, with the idea of greater local control and deference to on-the-spot Scottish views. Much of the support for Scottish home rule had been buoyed up by the current revival of the Irish question, but there is no doubt either that the Liberal MPs who were pressing the topic before 1914 had much of the popular sentiment of their constituents behind them. The idea had been sustained consistently ever since 1886 and had won its way in the Liberal party despite the earlier reservations of the party managers. There seems to have been a widespread expectation that once the Irish Home Rule Act of 1912 had passed the Lords suspensory veto, a local parliament would follow in Scotland in some federal scheme.[34]

There were solid grounds, too, for arguing that there was a society distinct enough in Scotland to merit such treatment. While the economic, social and cultural forces of modernisation had affected the people of Britain in broadly the same way, the resulting mixtures of urban and rural balances, of economic concentration and opportunity, of administrative response and development had depended very much on geographical circumstances and previous history. With the growing role of the state in everyday lives, the physical and psychological distance from Westminster and Whitehall was becoming more of a problem. Scotland's experience of a century of change had not been the same as England's. Its history had continued to be different, much of it shaped by the distinctive nature of its terrain and much by the social composition and conditions of its people. Scotland's 19.5 million acres were mostly made up of mountains, heath and rough grazing, with only 4.5 million of arable. It had a land problem on its northwestern fringes like that of the west of Ireland, while in the glens and valleys abutting on its eastern Grampians it resembled more the agriculture of Scandinavia. Lowland farming was prosperous due to highly prized stock and crop specialisms. The eastern fisheries had the characteristics of a large-scale industry more like its English counterparts than the smaller inshore fishing ventures on the west. While most of the land mass was thinly populated, the bulk of the population was crammed into a stifling, vast, Ruhr-like industrial complex in the narrow belt between the Clyde and the Forth. Its urban balance was quite unlike that of England's, however, so that any scheme of administration devised for the latter would have to be seriously modified to suit Scottish conditions. England had over sixty large cities with populations in excess of 50 000, while Scotland had only nine, the great bulk of the remaining burghs being well below the 20 000 level. Its Irish component played a larger role relative to the rest of the population, while its Gaelic-speaking Highlanders represented an element not found in industrial England. Its urban and rural land laws faced housing and tenure conditions which were unique not only in Britain but Europe. There seemed to be a greater commitment to public provision of services, perhaps because the pace of its urbanisation had overwhelmed the simple local models in existence at the start of the century. This was particularly evident in education, where the local state provided most of it, with only a fraction in voluntary schools. This meant that any solution to the 'dual' system was likely to work out differently in Scotland, where it was largely a question of how to deal with a minority, as compared with England where the existence of a large, mainly Anglican, sector did not provide the same opportunities. In Scotland in 1901, there were 2799 board and only 353 voluntary schools, compared with 5878 board and 14 275 voluntary schools in England. It was this balance which determined that in any future development of the system the Roman Catholics in Scotland would have to cede outright control of their schools in return for some guarantee as to their religious character and become integrated into the public sector. Even before the 1918 Education Act accomplished this, the Scotch Education Department and the larger school boards were making moves in this direction in 1911. In

1872 the Roman Catholics had not mattered all that much because the Act had been aimed at other priorities concerning the bulk of the country's children. However, their small number of only 65 schools in 1872 had grown rapidly to 92 in 1875, 179 in 1895 and 220 by 1910 in a constant effort to keep up with the standards demanded by the host society. By then, forward-looking administrators like Sir John Struthers were determined to bring that group up to the standards and opportunities enjoyed by the rest of the country.[35]

Such moves were expressions of a society with some belief in itself, not one fearful of its future. Scottish life and institutions have been regarded as becoming less confident and resilient after 1800 under the pressure of economic and social change, especially in comparison with its great age of Enlightenment. Considering the suddenness with which its was assailed by the forces of industrialisation after 1800, with layer upon layer of new developments up to about 1870, in fact it survived remarkably well. After more than a century of fundamental transformation within Great Britain, Scotland still retained a strong sense of its own identity, with values derived from that experience of change. Partly this was due to the confidence gained from being part of that wider Empire and of having played a part in its development out of proportion to its own size, not only in military contribution but in a range of industrial output which had literally made Scotland the workshop of the new world of iron and steam. Its loyalties to the symbols of the British state were confidently shared with the rest of Britain, but it was still conscious of itself as a distinct and different part of the island. Despite frictions, it had managed to absorb new elements from Ireland into its urban development, as well as the new groups of Scots who had migrated from the countryside. There was a growing realisation of the considerable backlog of social need that still required to be addressed, especially in housing and labour conditions. The crofting communities had been stabilised to some extent, but largely only as a holding operation, and questions still remained as to their future resiliency. While all the great nineteenth-century staples were represented in its economy, the growing dominance of cartels and the uncertainties of international markets were increasingly posing questions as to the overrepresentation of these staples, and the future of the many small businesses who supplied and serviced them. In public ethos and institutions there was a sense that the ladders of opportunity had been maintained, and that professional expertise and a bias toward the humanities still gave a tone to the educational system. Victorian and Edwardian Scotland appeared to have little by way of institutions or symbols which repre-sented it in a tangible form. But there was an underlying belief that it stood for progress based on moral fairness, an idea of common equality and destiny and concern for religious values which can be traced back to the sixteenth century and beyond to its middle ages. The universal rush to join the colours in August 1914 showed that there was a Scotland worth defending, if not as a state then as a culture in which its diverse and often contrasting regions could find some common expression.

# NOTES AND REFERENCES

## Abbreviations

IR        *Innes Review*
JSLHS     *Journal of the Scottish Labour History Society*
PP        *Parliamentary Papers*
RSCHS     *Records of the Scottish Church History Society*
SESH      *Scottish Economic and Social History*
SHR       *Scottish Historical Review*
SHS       *Scottish History Society*

## 1  A SOCIETY IN TRANSITION: 1800–32

1. T. Devine, 'Urbanisation', in T. M. Devine and R. Mitchison (eds), *People and Society in Scotland I 1760–1830* (Edinburgh, 1988), pp. 28–9.
2. *The Statistical Account of Scotland*, compiled 1791–9, provides an invaluable 'snapshot' of each of Scotland's 938 parishes at a period of crucial change. It is generally referred to as the *'Old' Statistical Account* to distinguish it from a later, similar survey of 1834–45, the *'New' Statistical Account*, with which it may be usefully compared as to the extent of change experienced during this period.
3. M. Gray, *Scots On The Move. Scots Migrants 1750–1914* (The Economic and Social History Society of Scotland, 1990); M. W. Flinn (ed.), *Scottish Population History from the Seventeenth Century to the 1930s* (Cambridge, 1977), pp. 461–5.
4. A. Somerville, *The Autobiography of a Working Man* (reprinted, London, 1951); M. Robson, 'The Border Farm Worker', in T. M. Devine (ed.), *Farm Servants and Labour in Scotland 1770–1914* (Edinburgh, 1984), p. 91; *PP. Factory Inquiry 1833. 1st Report. Mins of Evidence*, p. 104; F. S. Buchanan (ed.), *A Good Time Coming. Mormon Letters to Scotland* (Salt Lake City, 1988), pp. xxi, 16.
5. Flinn, *Scottish Population History*, pp. 441–55; R. A. Cage (ed.), *The Scots Abroad* (London, 1985).

6.  C. W. J. Withers, *Gaelic in Scotland 1698–1981* (Edinburgh, 1984), pp. 184–7, 198–203; Flinn, *Scottish Population History*, p. 425.
7.  By 1878, there were many more Roman Catholics in Scotland than Irish-bom (some 332 600 or 9.2 per cent of the population – see J. Darragh, 'The Catholic population of Scotland 1878–1977', *IR*, xxix (1978), pp. 229–30), indicating the growing size of a Scoto-Irish second generation of immigrants after 1850.
8.  J. E. Handley, *The Irish in Scotland* (Cork, 1945) and *The Irish in Modern Scotland* (Cork, 1947); R. Swift and S. Gilley (eds), *The Irish in the Victorian City* (London, 1985); C. Johnson, *Developments in the Roman Catholic Church in Scotland 1789–1829* (Edinburgh, 1983), pp. 222–3.
9.  *PP. State of the Irish Poor In Great Britain, Appendix G. 1836*, p. 118.
10. M. L. Parry and T. R. Slater (eds), *The Making of the Scottish Countryside* (London, 1980); also, M. Gray, 'Scottish emigration: the social impact of agrarian change in the rural lowlands, 1775–1875', in *Perspectives in American History*, VIII (1973), pp. 112–44, and 'The social impact of agricultural change in the rural lowlands', in Devine and Mitchison, *People and Society I*, pp. 53–69; T. Devine, *The Transformation of Rural Scotland: Social Change and the Agrarian Economy, 1600–1815* (Edinburgh, 1994); J. A. Symon, *Scottish Farming Past and Present* (Edinburgh, 1959) provides a useful overall account.
11. Somerville, *Autobiography*, p. 44; W. Donaldson, *Popular Literature in Victorian Scotland* (Aberdeen, 1984), p. 14; P. B. Freshwater (ed.), *Sons of Scotia, Raise your Voice* (Edinburgh, 1991); C. A. Whatley, 'Women, girls and vitriolic song': a note on the Glasgow cotton strike of 1825', *JSLHS*, 28 (1993), pp. 71–6; R. H. Campbell, 'The Landed Classes', in Devine and Mitchison, *People and Society I*, pp. 91–108.
12. J. Hunter, *The Making of the Crofting Community* (Edinburgh, 1976); T. M. Devine, *The Great Highland Famine* (Edinburgh, 1988).
13. T. M. Devine, *Clanship to Crofters' War* (Manchester, 1994), p. 68.
14. R. H. Campbell, *Scotland since 1707* (2nd edn, Edinburgh, 1985); B. P. Lenman, *An Economic History of Modern Scotland* (London, 1977); A. Slaven, *The Development of the West of Scotland: 1750–1960* (London, 1975).
15. Sir J. Sinclair, *Analysis of the Statistical Account of Scotland*, 2 vols (Edinburgh, 1825, reprinted New York and London, 1970), I, 207.
16. Sir A. Alison, *Some Account of My Life and Writings*, 2 vols (Edinburgh, 1883), I, 344–6; noted also for his *History of Europe* and as the brother of the medical and poor law reformer, William Pulteney Alison, whose social philosophy he shared, as in his anti-Malthusian essay, *Principles of Population* (1840).
17. Elizabeth Grant of Rothiemurchus, *Memoirs of a Highland Lady*, 2 vols, ed. A. Tod (Edinburgh, 1988), II, 104–5; Alison, *My Life*, I, 344–5.
18. M. Ash, *The Strange Death of Scottish History* (Edinburgh, 1980); C. Kidd, *Subverting Scotland's Past* (Cambridge, 1993).
19. W. H. Fraser, *Conflict and Class. Scottish Workers 1700–1838* (Edinburgh, 1988); T. Clarke and T. Dickson, 'The birth of class?', in Devine and Mitchison, *People and Society I*, pp. 292–309.

20. W. Ferguson, *Scotland 1689 to the Present* (Edinburgh, reprint, 1978), pp. 266ff.; R. M. W. Cowan, *The Newspaper in Scotland 1815–1860* (Glasgow, 1946).

21. F. Montgomery, 'Glasgow and the movement for corn law repeal', *History*, lxiv (1979), pp. 363–79. Fraser, *Conflict and Class*, pp. 89–96; H. W. Meikle, *Scotland and the French Revolution* (Glasgow, 1912), p. 220.

22. W. M. Roach, 'Radical reform movements in Scotland from 1815 to 1822', University of Glasgow, Ph.D. Thesis, 1970.

23. Fraser, *Conflict and Class*, pp. 111–3; see also the assessment of this episode in M. I. Thomis and P. Holt, *Threats of Revolution in Britain 1789–1848* (London, 1977).

24. A. L. Drummond and J. Bulloch, *The Scottish Church 1688–1843* (Edinburgh, 1973), pp. 151ff. For a case study of the forces at work, see I. F. Maciver, 'Unfinished business? The Highland churches' scheme and the government of Scotland, 1818–1835', *RSCHS*, xxv (1995), pp. 376–99.

25. *Case of the Operative Cotton-spinners in Glasgow* (Glasgow, 1825), p. 23; F. A. Montgomery, 'The unstamped press: the contribution of Glasgow, 1831–1836', *SHR*, LIX (1980), pp. 154–70.

26. W. Ferguson, 'The Electoral System in the Scottish Counties before 1832', *Stair Society Miscellany II*, 35 (1984), pp. 261–94.

27. M. Dyer, *Men of Property and Intelligence. The Scottish Electoral System prior to 1884* (Aberdeen, 1996), pp. 15–17; J. Brooke, *The House of Commons 1754–1790: Introductory Survey* (Oxford, 1964), pp. 62–7; I. Maver, 'The guardianship of the community: civic authority before 1833', in T. M. Devine and G. Jackson (eds), *Glasgow Volume I: Beginnings to 1830* (Manchester, 1995), p. 261.

28. By about 50 per cent if the traditional figure of 435 000 is used for the 1831 electorate: by about 80 per cent if the revised figure of 366 000 is accepted; see M. Brock, *The Great Reform Act* (London, 1973), p. 312. Also, I. G. C. Hutchison, *A Political History of Scotland 1832–1924* (Edinburgh, 1986), p. 1.

29. W. Ferguson, 'The Reform Act (Scotland) of 1832: intention and effect', *SHR*, XLV (1966), pp. 105–14; M. Dyer, ' "Mere detail and machinery": the Great Reform Act and the effects of redistribution on Scottish representation, 1832–1868', *SHR*, XLII (1983), pp. 17–34; Dyer, *Men of Property*, pp. 31–47.

30. R. M. Urquhart, *The Burghs of Scotland and The Burgh Police (Scotland) Act 1833* (1985), pp. 39, 75, 98–9; For a comparative view, see J. Prest, *Liberty and Locality. Parliament, Permissive Legislation and Ratepayers' Democracies* (Oxford, 1990).

31. Urquhart, *Burghs of Scotland*, p. 31; S. C. Oliver, 'The administration of urban society in Scotland 1800–50, with reference to the growth of civic government in Glasgow and its suburbs', University of Glasgow, Ph.D. Thesis, 1995, pp. 167–8, 216.

32. *The Journal of Henry Cockburn 1831–1854*, 2 vols (Edinburgh, 1874), I, p. 54; W. H. Marwick, 'Municipal politics in Victorian Edinburgh', *Book of the Old Edinburgh Club*, xxxiii (1969), pp. 31–41; Maver, 'The guardianship of the community', in Devine and Jackson, *Glasgow Volume I*, pp. 268–70.

33. *Journal of Henry Cockburn*, II, 134–5.

## 2 A NEW SOCIETY: 1832–50

1. J. M. Wilson (ed.), *The Imperial Gazetteer of Scotland*, 2 vols (London, ?1866), II, 439–40.
2. Slaven, *Development of the West of Scotland*, pp. 113–25; Campbell, *Scotland since 1707*, pp. 95–105.
3. Slaven, *Development of the West of Scotland*, pp. 125ff.
4. C. J. A. Robertson, *The Origins of the Scottish Railway System 1722–1844* (Edinburgh, 1983); *The Railways of Scotland. Papers of Andrew C. O'Dell*, ed. by R. E. H. Mellor (Centre for Scottish Studies, University of Aberdeen); W. Vamplew, 'Railways and the transformation of the Scottish economy', *Economic History Review*, 2nd series, xxiv (1971), pp. 39–54; Lenman, *Economic History of Modern Scotland*, p. 172.
5. Lenman, *Economic History of Modern Scotland*, pp. 182–8; B. Lenman, *From Esk to Tweed: Harbours, Ships and Men of the East Coast of Scotland* (London, 1975).
6. N. Murray, *The Scottish Hand Loom Weavers 1790–1850: a Social History* (Edinburgh, 1978), pp. 23, 71, 93ff.; Slaven, *Development of West of Scotland*, p. 158; R. Rodger, 'Employment, wages and poverty in the Scottish cities 1841–1914', in G. Gordon (ed.), *Perspectives of the Scottish City* (Aberdeen, 1985), pp. 25–63; I. Levitt and C. Smout (eds), *The State of the Scottish Working-Class in 1843* (Edinburgh, 1979), pp. 259–63.
7. Campbell, *Scotland since 1707*, pp. 142ff.; Slaven, *Development of West of Scotland*, pp. 147–54. *PP. Sanitary Inquiry: Local Reports. Scotland. 1842*, pp. 315–6, 325; G. Cruickshank (ed.), *A Sense of Place. Studies in Scottish Local History* (Edinburgh, 1988), p. 90.
8. James Taylor, *The Annals of Fenwick*, ed. T. D. Taylor (Ayrshire Archaeological and Natural History Society, 1970), *passim; Glasgow Evening Post*, 19 and 26 September 1835; *Scottish Temperance Journal*, February 1841 and July 1844.
9. S. Mechie, *The Church and Scottish Social Development 1780–1870* (London, 1960), pp. 81–99; A. Wilson, *The Chartist Movement in Scotland* (Manchester, 1970), pp. 126–36, 256–8; James Hunter, *For The People's Cause. From the Writings of John Murdoch* (Edinburgh, 1986), pp. 18, 69; W. H. Fraser, 'Owenite Socialism in Scotland', *SESH*, 16 (1996), pp. 65–6.
10. R. M. Urquhart, *The Burghs of Scotland and The Police of Towns (Scotland) Act 1850* (1987), pp. 4–7, 55; F. McKichan, 'A burgh's response to the problems of urban growth: Stirling, 1780–1880', *SHR*, LVII (1978), pp. 68–86.
11. I. F. Maciver, 'Cockburn and the Church', in A. Bell (ed.), *Lord Cockburn A Bicentenary Commemoration 1779–1979* (Edinburgh, 1979), pp. 91–5. For a clear overview of the events and issues, see S. J. Brown's essay in S. J. Brown and M. Fry (eds), *Scotland in the Age of the Disruption* (Edinburgh, 1993), and F. Lyall, *Of Presbyters and Kings. Church and State in the Law of Scotland* (Aberdeen, 1980).
12. The original area of the city north of the Clyde which did not include the surrounding areas of Calton and Anderston.
13. Drummond and Bulloch, *The Scottish Church*, pp. 246ff.; S. J. Brown, *Thomas Chalmers and the Godly Commonwealth* (Oxford, 1982), pp. 334ff.

14. Hutchison, *Political History of Scotland*, pp. 59–65. Withers, *Gaelic in Scotland*, p. 174 notes that 101 out of the Church's 201 Gaelic-speaking ministers left to join the Free Church in 1843. See also Hunter, *Making of the Crofting Community*, pp. 103–6.
15. Handley, *Irish in Modern Scotland*, pp. 20–46; B. Collins, 'The origins of Irish immigration to Scotland', in T. M. Devine (ed.), *Irish Immigrants and Scottish Society in the Nineteenth and Twentieth Centuries* (Edinburgh, 1991), pp. 1–18.
16. B. Aspinwall, 'The formation of the Catholic community in the west of Scotland', *IR*, xxxiii (1982), pp. 44–57; J. F. McCaffrey, 'Irish immigrants and radical movements in the west of Scotland in the early nineteenth century', *IR*, xxxix (1988), pp. 46–60; *Glasgow Herald*, 9 July 1852.
17. W. P. Alison, *Observations on the Famine of 1846–7 in the Highlands of Scotland and in Ireland* (Edinburgh, 1847).
18. Devine, *Highland Famine*, pp. 180–1.
19. Ibid., p. 329; Flinn, *Population History*, p. 437, suggests that the Famine led to an outflow from the west Highlands and Islands 'of almost one-third of their pre-famine numbers, or possibly 60 000 people'.
20. Yeon-Soo Oh, 'Poor relief in Scotland before 1850', University of Aberdeen, Ph.D. Thesis, 1995, p. 257. For Alison see J. H. F. Brotherston, 'William Pulteney Alison, Scottish pioneer of social medicine', *The Medical Officer*, 6 June 1958, pp. 331–6.
21. *PP. Poor Laws in Scotland. Report. 1844*, pp. xviii–lxiv.
22. Yeon-Soo Oh, 'Poor relief in Scotland', pp. 354–6.
23. A. Paterson, 'The poor law in ninetenth-century Scotland', in D. Fraser (ed.), *The New Poor Law in the Nineteenth Century* (London, 1976), pp. 171–93; *PP. Select Committee Scottish Poor Law. 1870*, pp. x–xii; W. Groves, 'The administration of the poor law in Lanarkshire 1845–1894' (University of Glasgow, Ph. D. Thesis, 1990) is a valuable regional study.
24. A. Tyrrell, 'Political economy, whiggism and the education of working-class adults in Scotland 1817–40', *SHR*, XLVIII (1969), pp. 151–65; B. Hilton, 'Chalmers as political economist', in A. C. Cheyne (ed.), *The Practical and the Pious. Essays on Thomas Chalmers (1780–1847)* (Edinburgh, 1985), pp. 141–156.
25. Fraser, *Conflict and Class*, pp. 153ff.; W. H. Marwick, *A Short History of Labour in Scotland* (Edinburgh, 1967), pp. 14–34.
26. A. B. Campbell, *The Lanarkshire Miners* (Edinburgh, 1979), pp. 49ff.; G. M. Wilson, *Alexander McDonald, Leader of the Miners* (Aberdeen, 1982), pp. 30–56.
27. Wilson, *Chartist Movement in Scotland, passim*; R. Duncan, 'Chartism in Aberdeen: radical politics and culture 1838–48', in T. Brotherstone (ed.), *Covenant, Charter, and Party* (Aberdeen, 1989), pp. 78–91.
28. *Chartist Circular*, 20 Feburary 1841; *Northern Star*, 3 July 1847.
29. Wilson, *Chartist Movement*, pp. 255–67; W. H. Fraser, 'Trade unions, reform and the election of 1868 in Scotland', *SHR*, L (1971), pp. 149–56.
30. Dyer, *Men of Property*, pp. 53, 65.
31. Hutchison, *Political History of Scotland*, p. 38.
32. Ibid., p. 25. 'I have been led to the conclusion that the tenantry of Scotland are, on the whole, very indifferent to points of mere civil politics. . . . But in

this Church question, I am firmly persuaded that the influence of the land-lords will be absolutely nothing over those who are Non-Intrusionists. On points which involve religious and Presbyterian principles, the tenantry of Scotland will be found as inflexible as their forefathers.' A. Thomson of Banchory to Lord Aberdeen, 14 August 1841, quoted in Lady Frances Balfour, *Life of the 4th Earl of Aberdeen* (1922), p. 92.

33. Hutchison, *Political History of Scotland*, p. 62ff.; G. F. Millar, 'The Liberal party in Scotland, 1843–1868', University of Glasgow, Ph.D. Thesis, 1994, pp. 52–3, 67–76, 343ff.

34. For the new type of men, see J. B. Mackie, *The Life and Work of Duncan McLaren* 2 vols (Edinburgh, 1888); A. Nicolson, *Memoirs of Adam Black* (Edinburgh, 1885); D. Keir, *The House of Collins* (London, 1952).

35. K. J. Cameron, 'Anti-corn law agitations in Scotland, with particular reference to the Anti-Corn League' (University of Edinburgh, Ph.D. Thesis, 1971) is the basic work on this topic; see also K. J. Cameron, 'William Weir and the origins of the "Manchester League" in Scotland, 1833–39', *SHR*, LVIII (1979), pp. 70–91.

36. Cowan, *Newspaper in Scotland*, pp. 201ff.

37. Cameron, 'Anti-corn law agitations', *passim; Glasgow Argus*, 13, 14, 17 January 1842.

38. *Scotsman*, 14 July 1847.

39. Hutchison, *Political History of Scotland*, p. 90; J. I. Brash (ed.), *Papers on Scottish Electoral Politics 1832–1854, SHS*, 4th series, 11 (1974), pp. lxii–lxiii; Millar, 'Liberal Party in Scotland', pp. 163ff., provides a detailed picture of the Conservative decline in the counties.

## 3   NORTH BRITAIN: 1850–86

1. Lenman, *Economic History of Modern Scotland*, pp. 173–93.

2. W. Donaldson, 'Popular literature: the press, the people and the vernacular revival', in D. Gifford (ed.), *The History of Scottish Literature, Volume 3 Nineteenth Century* (Aberdeen, 1988), pp. 203–15.

3. Ash, *Strange Death of Scottish History*, pp. 59–86; T. Duffy, 'George A. Griffin: a priest among antiquaries', *IR*, xxvii (1976), pp. 127–61.

4. H. J. Hanham, *Scottish Nationalism* (London, 1969), pp. 54, 74ff.

5. *Address To The People of Scotland and Statement of Grievances* (Edinburgh, 1853), pp. 14–30; H. J. Hanham, 'Mid-century Scottish nationalism, romantic and radical', in R. Robson (ed.), *Ideas and Institutions of Victorian Britain* (London, 1967), pp. 143–79.

6. Sinclair, *Analysis of Statistical Account*, part I, Appendix, pp. 68–71. *Journal of Henry Cockburn*, I, 125–7. University of Glasgow, David Murray Collection: *Scotland Interested in the Question of Federal or Local Parliaments By A Scotchman* (Glasgow, 1844). I thank Professor J. G. Kellas for drawing my attention to this.

7. G. White, 'David Livingstone In Search of Beauty', *Scottish Geographical Magazine*, lxxxix (1973), pp. 157–61; A. MacGillivray, 'Exile and Empire', in Gifford, *History of Scottish Literature*, p. 424, quotes Livingstone speaking of 'my principles as an Englishman'. C. Kidd, 'Teutonist ethnology and Scottish nationalist inhibition, 1780–1880', *SHR*, LXXIV (1995), p. 72. For this theme in general, see R. Finlay, 'The rise and fall of popular imperialism in Scotland, 1850–1950', *Scottish Geographical Magazine*, 113 (1997), pp. 13–21.

8. Hunter, *For the People's Cause*, pp. 99–101.

9. J. Fyfe (ed.), *Autobiography of John McAdam (1806–1883)*, *SHS*, 4th series, 16 (1980), p. xviii; J. Fyfe, 'Scottish volunteers with Garibaldi', *SHR*, LVII (1978), pp. 168–81.

10. Mitchell Library, Glasgow, manuscripts: E151243 S.R. 207, William Wallace Memorial Papers and Accounts.

11. D. J. Withrington, 'Schooling, literacy and society', in Devine and Mitchison, *People and Society I*, pp. 184–5; R. D. Anderson, *Education and the Scottish People 1750–1918* (Oxford, 1995), pp. 89–99.

12. J. D. Myers, 'Scottish nationalism and the antecedents of the 1872 Education Act', *Scottish Educational Studies*, 4 (1972), p. 75.

13. Anderson, *Education and the Scottish People*, pp. 50–57; Hutchison, *Political History of Scotland*, pp. 70–83.

14. Myers, 'Scottish nationalism', p. 79.

15. W. H. Fraser and I. Maver, 'Tackling the problems', in W. H. Fraser and I. Maver (eds), *Glasgow Volume II: 1830 to 1912* (Manchester, 1996), pp. 417–8.

16. R. M. Urquhart, *The Burghs of Scotland and the General Police Improvement (Scotland) Act 1862*, 2 Parts (Motherwell, 1991), pp. 385–93, 431–3; G. Gordon, *Perspectives of the Scottish City* (Aberdeen, 1985); R. J. Morris, 'Urbanisation and Scotland', in W. H. Fraser and R. J. Morris (eds), *People and Society in Scotland II*, 1830–1914 (Edinburgh, 1990), p. 97; R. J. Naismith, *The Story of Scotland's Towns* (Edinburgh, 1989), pp. 118ff.

17. A. Gibb, *Glasgow. The Making Of A City* (London, 1983), p. 143; J. Butt, 'Working class housing in the Scottish cities 1900–1950', in G. Gordon and B. Dicks (eds), *Scottish Urban History* (Aberdeen, 1983), p. 237; W. H. Fraser and I. Maver, 'The social problems of the city', in *Glasgow Volume II*, p. 365.

18. I. Levitt, 'The poor law and unemployment' in T. C. Smout (ed.), *The Search for Wealth and Statibility* (London, 1979); Groves, 'Administration of the poor law in Lanarkshire', pp. 67, 305.

19. M. Gemmell, *The Societies of Glasgow* (Glasgow, 1908).

20. Anderson, *Education and the Scottish People*, pp. 57–72; D. J. Withrington, 'Towards a national system, 1867–72', *Scottish Educational Studies*, 4 (1972), pp. 107–24; R. D. Anderson, *Education and Opportunity in Victorian Scotland* (Oxford, 1983), *passim*.

21. Anderson, *Education and the Scottish People*, pp. 181–2, 261–5 and *passim*.

22. The small role of the voluntary sector in Scotland, however, consisting mainly of these Catholic schools, made their eventual integration into the public sector more likely. See Chapter 5 below and J. C. Stocks, 'Church and state in Britain: the legacy of the 1870s', *History of Education*, 25 (1996),

pp. 211–22. T. A. Fitzpatrick, *Catholic Secondary Education in South-west Scotland Before 1972* (Aberdeen, 1986), pp. 29–40.

23. Anderson, *Education and Opportunity*, pp. 339–40.
24. Millar, 'Liberal party in Scotland', pp. 175–214; Hutchison, *Political History of Scotland*, pp. 90, 103–6.
25. Fraser, 'Trade unions, reform and the 1868 election', p. 144; I. MacDougall (ed.), *The Minutes of Edinburgh Trades Council 1859–1873, SHS*, 4th series, 5 (1968), pp. xxvii–xxix.
26. J. K. Walton, *The Second Reform Act* (London, 1987), p. 19.
27. Dyer, *Men of Property and Intelligence*, pp. 109–20.
28. Hutchison, *Political History of Scotland*, pp. 109–19.
29. C. G. Brown, *The Social History of Religion in Scotland since 1730* (London, 1987), p. 64; J. G. Kellas, 'The Liberal party and the Scottish church disestablishment crisis', *English Historical Review*, LXXIX (1964), pp. 31–46.
30. R. Kelley, 'Midlothian: a study in politics and ideas', *Victorian Studies*, 4 (1960), pp. 119–40.
31. Hutchison, *Political History*, pp. 141ff.; M. Dyer, *Capable Citizens and Improvident Democrats. The Scottish Electoral System 1884–1929* (Aberdeen, 1996), pp. 11–18.
32. A. C. Cheyne, 'Church reform and church defence: the contribution of Principal John Tulloch (1823–1886)', *RSCHS*, xxxii (1989), p. 416; *Scottish Council of the Liberation Society. Sixth Annual Report 1884*, p. 17.
33. *Scotsman*, 27 May 1885.
34. G. I. T. Machin, *Politics and the Churches in Great Britain 1869 to 1921* (Oxford, 1987), p. 146.
35. *Glasgow Herald*, 29 September and 21 October, 1885; J. G. Kellas, 'The Liberal party in Sotland 1876–1895', *SHR*, XLIV (1965), pp. 6–7.
36. Kellas, ibid., p. 10; J. F. McCaffrey, 'The origins of Liberal Unionism in the west of Scotland', *SHR*, L (1971), pp. 47–71.
37. Quoted in *North British Daily Mail*, 21 April 1886.
38. J. F. McCaffrey, 'Politics and the Catholic community since 1878', *IR*, xxix (1978), pp. 146–9.
39. Hunter, *Making of the Crofting Community*, pp. 131–54; I. M. M. MacPhail, *The Crofters' War* (Stornoway, 1989), pp. 88ff.
40. *Glasgow Herald*, 7 November 1885; C. Levy, 'Conservatism and Liberal Unionism in Glasgow 1874–1912', University of Dundee, Ph.D. Thesis, 1983), p. 298ff.
41. R. Douglas, *Land, People & Politics* (London, 1976), pp. 47, 72; J. D. Young, *The Rousing of the Scottish Working Class* (London, 1979), pp. 148–55.
42. J. Mavor, *My Windows on the Street of the World*, 2 vols (London and Toronto, 1923), I, 174–7.
43. F. Reid, *Keir Hardie. The Making of A Socialist* (London, 1978), pp. 46ff.
44. 'Scottish Liberals are Liberals not so much of their deliberate choice, as because Liberalism has been for half a century the atmosphere they breathed. They were born into it.' *Scotland at the General Election of 1885 by A Tory Democrat* (Edinburgh, 1885), p. 10.
45. *The National Meeting in Favour of a Separate Department of State for Scotland held in Edinburgh January 1884* (reprinted Edinburgh, 1900); H. J. Hanham,

'The Creation of the Scottish Office, 1881–87', *The Juridical Review*, 10 (December 1965), pp. 205–44.

46. James Bryce warned Gladstone that Scottish home rule implied changing the British constitution ultimately to a form of federalism. He also felt that demand for home rule was growing because Scotland wanted more radical measures than the English Conservative majority in Parliament would concede. Bodleian Library, MS Bryce 11, fol. 158, Bryce to W. E. Gladstone, 22 December 1886, and MS Bryce 12, fol. 101–2, Bryce to Gladstone, 5 December 1892.

## 4  REALIGNMENTS: 1886–1900

1. Slaven, *Development of the West of Scotland*, pp. 166ff.; Campbell, *Scotland since 1707*, pp. 171ff.
2. C. Lee, 'Aberdeen 1800–2000 AD', in T. Brotherstone and D. J. Withrington (eds), *The City and its Worlds. Aspects of Aberdeen's History since 1794* (Glasgow, 1996), pp. 211–23; Lenman, *Economic History of Modern Scotland*, p. 197; M. McCarthy, *Social Geography of Paisley* (Paisley, 1969), p. 99.
3. C. H. Lee, 'Modern economic growth and structural change in Scotland: the service sector reconsidered', *SESH*, 3 (1983), p. 7.
4. Campbell, *Scotland since 1707*, p. 183.
5. Lee, 'Modern economic growth and the service sector', pp. 9–23; Rodger, 'Employment, wages and poverty', Gordon, *Perspectives of the Scottish City*, pp. 42–6.
6. J. H. Treble, *Urban Poverty in Britain 1830–1914* (London, 1979), pp. 185–9; Slaven, *Development of the West of Scotland*, pp. 243–4, 255–7; Devine, *Clanship to Crofters' War*, pp. 232–9; E. A. Cameron, 'Politics, ideology and the Highland land issue, 1886 to the 1920s', *SHR*, LXXII (1993), pp. 60–79.
7. W. H. Fraser, 'Developments in leisure', in Fraser and Morris, *People and Society II*, pp. 244–61.
8. I. Levitt, *Government and Social Conditions in Scotland 1845–1919, SHS*, 5th series, 1 (1988), pp. xvii–xxxv; I. H. Adams, *The Making of Urban Scotland* (London, 1978), pp. 161–4; J. S. Gibson, *The Thistle and The Crown. A History of the Scottish Office* (Edinburgh, 1985), p. 33.
9. R. Rodger, 'Crisis and confrontation in Scottish housing, 1880–1914', in R. Rodger (ed.), *Scottish Housing in the Twentieth Century* (Leicester, 1989), pp. 26–9.
10. Rodger, ibid., pp. 39–42; Fraser and Maver, 'Social problems of the city', *Glasgow Volume II*, pp. 372–8.
11. Rodger, 'Employment, wages and poverty', Gordon, *Perspectives of the Scottish City*, pp. 47–9.

12. W. M. Walker, *Juteopolis. Dundee and its Textile Workers 1885–1923* (Edinburgh, 1979), pp. 85–93.
13. H. George, *Progress and Poverty* (1880; Everyman edn, 1911), pp. 9–10; Also Reid, *Keir Hardie*, p. 97.
14. D. J. Withrington, 'The churches in Scotland, *c.*1870–*c.*1900: towards a new social conscience?', *RSCHS*, xix (1977), pp. 155–68; and A. C. Cheyne, *The Transforming of the Kirk* (Edinburgh, 1983), pp. 130–45. S. J. Brown, 'The social vision of Scottish Presbyterianism and the Union of 1929', *RSCHS*, xxiv (1990), pp. 79–83.
15. Sir H. Jones and J. H. Muirhead, *Life and Philosophy of Edward Caird* (1921), p. 198.
16. E. Caird, *The Moral Aspects of the Economical Problem* (1888), pp. 8–9.
17. Jones and Muirhead, *Life of Caird*, pp. 115–25.
18. Biographical sketch by Thomas Jones in W. Smart, *Second Thoughts of an Economist* (London, 1916), pp. xv–xxxv; see Young, *Rousing of the Scottish Working Class*, p. 150, for an example of Smart's influence.
19. Reid, *Keir Hardie*, p. 115.
20. National Library of Scotland, MS Dep. 176/vol 8. Hardie to H. Champion, March 1888.
21. D. Howell, *British Workers and the Independent Labour Party 1888–1906* (Manchester, 1983), pp. 33, 146–7; W. H. Fraser, 'Trade councils in the Labour movement in nineteenth century Scotland' in I. MacDougall (ed.), *Essays in Scottish Labour History* (Edinburgh, 1979), pp. 1–28.
22. J. J. Smyth, 'The ILP in Glasgow, 1888–1906: the struggle for identity', in A. McKinlay and R. J. Morris (eds), *The ILP on Clydeside, 1893–1932: from Foundation to Disintegration* (Manchester, 1991), pp. 21–2, 45–6; I. S. Wood, 'John Wheatley, the Irish, and the Labour movement in Scotland', *IR*, xxxi (1980), p. 73; B. Aspinwall, 'The Catholic Irish and wealth in Glasgow', in Devine, *Irish Immigrants and Scottish Society*, pp. 94–6; Also J. F. McCaffrey, 'Irish issues in the nineteenth and twentieth centuries: radicalism in a Scottish context?', ibid., pp. 122–3; N. D. Denny, 'Temperance and the Scottish churches, 1870–1914', *RSCHS*, xxiii (1988), pp. 217–39.
23. Howell, *British Workers and the ILP*, pp. 146–8. The Party's constitution and programme are given in full in R. H. Campbell and J. B. A. Dow, *Source Book of Scottish Economic and Social History* (Oxford, 1968), pp. 208–10.
24. Howell, *British Workers and the ILP*, pp. 150–70 *passim*; R. Q. Gray, *The Labour Aristocracy in Victorian Edinburgh* (Oxford, 1976), p. 169ff.
25. M. Fry, *Patronage and Principle. A Political History of Modern Scotland* (Aberdeen, 1987), p. 115; Hutchison, *Political History of Scotland*, pp. 170–5.
26. D. Powell, 'The Liberal Ministries and Labour, 1892–1895', *History*, 68 (1983), pp. 369–93.
27. I. Levitt, *Poverty and Welfare in Scotland 1890–1948* (Edinburgh, 1988), pp. 23–4.
28. Hutchison, *Political History of Scotland*, pp. 176, 181–5.
29. Hutchison, ibid., pp. 202–7; S. J. Brown, '"Echoes of Midlothian": Scottish Liberalism and the South African War, 1899–1902', *SHR*, LXXI (1992), pp. 156–68.
30. Levitt, *Government and Social Conditions*, pp. xxxiv–xxxv, xli–xliii; Levitt, *Poverty and Welfare*, pp. 38–9.

31. D. J. Withrington, '"A ferment of change": aspirations, ideas and ideals in nineteenth century Scotland', in Gifford, *History of Scottish Literature*, pp. 54–9.

32. D. J. Withrington, 'Non-church-going, church organisation and "crisis in the church" *c*.1880–*c*.1920', *RSCHS*, xxiv (1991), pp. 199–219; R. Sjolinder, *Presbyterian Reunion in Scotland 1907–1921* (Edinburgh, ?1962), pp. 69–70; D. Watson, *Chords of Memory* (Edinburgh, 1936), pp. 33, 75–93.

33. L. S. Hunter, *John Hunter A Life* (London, 1922), pp. 116–7, 121–6.

34. Fraser and Maver, 'Social Problems of the City', in *Glasgow Volume II*, pp. 372–4, and 'Tackling the problems', ibid., pp. 422–3, 430–2; W. Smart, 'Discussion on "Housing Problems"', *Proceedings of the Royal Philosophical Society of Glasgow*, xxxiii (1901–2), pp. 3–21; B. Aspinwall, *Portable Utopia. Glasgow and The United States 1820–1920* (Aberdeen, 1984), pp. 154–7.

35. Mitchell Library Glasgow, Glasgow United Trades Council Annual Reports (microfilm), *Annual Report 1895–6*; W. H. Fraser, 'The Working Class', in *Glasgow Volume II*, pp. 337–8; Gray, *Labour Aristocracy in Victorian Edinburgh*, pp. 181–2; K. D. Buckley, *Trade Unionism in Aberdeen 1878 to 1900* (Edinburgh, 1955), pp. 178–80.

36. A. Tuckett, *The Scottish Trades Union Congress. The First 80 Years 1897–1977* (Edinburgh, 1986), p. 29; Howell, *British Workers and the ILP*, p. 171.

37. I. Wood, 'Irish immigrants and Scottish radicalism, 1880–1906', in MacDougall, *Essays in Scottish Labour History*, pp. 72–9.

38. J. Hunter, 'The Gaelic connection: the Highlands, Ireland and nationalism, 1873–1922', *SHR*, LIV (1975), pp. 178–85.

39. W. M. Walker, 'Irish immigrants in Scotland: their priests, politics and parochial life', *Historical Journal*, xv (1972), pp. 649–67; McCaffrey, 'Irish issues in the nineteenth and twentieth centuries', pp. 125–6.

40. Howell, *British Workers and the ILP*, pp. 165–6.

41. J. F. McCaffrey, 'The Roman Catholic church in the 1890s: retrospect and prospect', *RSCHS*, xxv (1995), pp. 426–41.

42. Brown, 'Scottish Liberalism and the South African War', pp. 165–8; *The Times*, 24 February, 2 March 1900.

43. Hutchison, *Political History of Scotland*, pp. 178–9.

44. Brown, 'Scottish Liberalism and the South African War', pp. 169–78.

5  NEW DIRECTIONS?: 1900–14

1. British Library, Campbell-Bannerman MSS, Add. MS 41252, fol. 234–43, Notes by W. Webster on Campbell-Bannerman's leadership. Webster had been the Organiser of the Western Division of the Scottish Liberal Association.

2. Brown, 'Scottish Liberalism and the South African War', pp. 173–81; Hutchison, *Political History of Scotland*, pp. 218–21.

3. Sjolinder, *Presbyterian Reunion*, pp. 107–16; Brown, 'The social vision of Scottish Presbyterianism', pp. 81–3.

4. A. K. Russell, *Liberal Landslide: the General Election of 1906* (Newton Abbot, 1973), pp. 106–8, 196–7.

5. Russell, ibid., pp. 65–77, 83–91, 172–207 *passim*.

6. Hutchison, *Political History of Scotland*, pp. 232–3, 250–6.

7. *Glasgow Herald*, 25 November 1905.

8. Levitt, *Poverty and Welfare*, pp. 50–1, 55–6.

9. Hutchison, *Political History of Scotland*, pp. 232–40.

10. Bodleian Library, Asquith MS 23, fol. 208–9, Alexander Murray to Asquith, 14 January 1910. For general economic aspects, see: J. H. Treble, 'Unemployment in Glasgow 1903–1910: Anatomy of a crisis', *JSLHS*, 25 (1990), pp. 8–39; J. H. Treble, 'The occupied male labour force', in Fraser and Morris, *People and Society II*, pp. 186–91; S. McKinstry, 'The Albion Motor Car Company: growth and specialisation 1899–1918', *SESH*, ll (1991), pp. 36–51.

11. Levitt, *Poverty and Welfare*, pp. 44–72, and *Government and Social Conditions*, pp. 99–101.

12. *Glasgow Herald*, 22 April 1909.

13. Levitt, *Government and Social Conditions*, pp. xlii–xliii.

14. Asquith MS 12, fol. 73, Alexander Murray to Asquith, 13 January 1910.

15. Rodger, 'Crisis and confrontation in Scottish housing', pp. 26–47; Levitt, *Government and Social Conditions*, pp. xxxiv–xxxv, 217–33.

16. Anderson, *Education and the Scottish People*, pp. 171, 208.

17. C. A. Whatley, 'Women and the economic transformation of Scotland *c.*1740–1830', *SESH*, 14 (1994), pp. 19–40; E. Gordon, *Women and the Labour Movement in Scotland, 1850–1914* (Oxford, 1991).

18. E. Gordon, 'Women's spheres', in Fraser and Morris, *People and Society II*, pp. 206–35; R. L. Bingham, 'The Glasgow Emancipation Society 1833–1876', University of Glasgow, M. Litt. Thesis, 1973; B. Aspinwall, 'Catholic teachers for Scotland: the Liverpool connection', *IR*, xlv (1994), pp. 47–70; I. Stewart, 'Teacher careers and the early Catholic schools of Edinburgh', *IR*, xlvi (1995), pp. 52–66.

19. D. Hutchison, *The Modern Scottish Theatre* (Glasgow, 1977), pp. 12–16.

20. C. W. Hill, *Edwardian Scotland* (Edinburgh, 1976), p. 61.

21. For instance, John Buchan, *Memory Hold The Door* (London, 1941), p. 147, but this older view has been superseded by the work of recent historians such as Dr Hutchison, Professor S. J. Brown and Dr Packer.

22. Hutchison, *Political History of Scotland*, pp. 256–65; Dyer, *Capable Citizens*, pp. 48, 76.

23. Hutchison, ibid., p. 262; Dyer, ibid., p. 98.

24. Howell, *British Workers and the ILP*, pp. 35–8; Asquith MS 23, fol. 298–300, J. A. Pease to Asquith, 24 October 1910, with enclosures on recent decisions on the Osborne Judgement by the Scottish Liberal Association and the Yorkshire Liberal Federation.

25. Walker, *Juteopolis*, pp. 343ff.

26. I. Packer, 'The land issue and the future of Scottish Liberalism in 1914', *SHR*, LXXV (1996), pp. 52–71; Hutchison, *Political History of Scotland*, pp. 242–5.

27. Marwick, *Short History of Labour*, pp. 78–83; R. Duncan and A. McIvor, *Militant Workers* (Edinburgh, 1992), pp. 81–105; Tuckett, *Scottish Trades Union Congress*, pp. 96–106.

28. J. Smith, 'Taking the leadership of the labour movement: the ILP in Glasgow, 1906–1914', in McKinlay and Morris, *The ILP on Clydeside*, pp. 60–70.

29. J. Melling, 'Clydeside rent struggles and the making of Labour politics in Scotland, 1900–39', in Rodger, *Scottish Housing in the Twentieth Century*, pp. 54–65.

30. R. McKibbin, *The Evolution of the Labour Party 1910–1924* (Oxford, 1974), pp. 7, 28–31, 39–42; Hutchison, *Political History of Scotland*, p. 254.

31. Hutchison, ibid., pp. 240–5; Packer, 'The land issue and Scottish Liberalism', pp. 64–5; Gibson, *The Thistle and The Crown*, pp. 53–4.

32. Smyth, 'The ILP in Glasgow, 1888–1906', in McKinlay and Morris, *The ILP on Clydeside*, pp. 45–7; Walker, *Juteopolis*, p. 62.

33. C. Harvie and G. Walker, 'Community and culture', in Fraser and Morris, *People and Society II*, pp. 336–57; Wood, 'John Wheatley, The Irish, and the Labour movement In Scotland', pp. 71–8; B. Aspinwall, 'The welfare state within the state: the Saint Vincent de Paul Society in Glasgow, 1848–1920', in W. J. Sheils and D. Wood (eds), *Voluntary Religion. Studies in Church History vol. 23* (Oxford, 1986), pp. 445–59.

34. Hanham, *Scottish Nationalism*, pp. 92–102; J. G. Kellas, *Modern Scotland* (London, rev. edn, 1980), pp. 96, 145.

35. G. S. Osborne, *Scottish and English Schools* (London, 1966), p. 11; Stocks, 'Church and state in Britain', pp. 217–8; Bro. Kenneth, 'The Education (Scotland) Act, 1918 in the making', *IR*, xix (1968), pp. 91–8.

# SELECT BIBLIOGRAPHY

What follows is highly selective, but most of the books cited contain extensive bibliographies of the many works on modern Scottish history that have appeared since the 1960s.

## GENERAL

Campbell, R. H., *Scotland Since 1707* (2nd edn, Edinburgh, 1985).
Checkland, S. and O., *Industry and Ethos. Scotland 1832–1914* (London, 1984).
Ferguson, W., *Scotland 1689 to the Present* (Edinburgh, 1978 edn).
Lenman, B., *Integration, Enlightenment, and Industrialization. Scotland 1746–1832* (London, 1981).
Lynch, M., *Scotland A New History* (London, 1991).
Smout, T. C., *A Century of the Scottish People 1830–1950* (London, 1986).

## POLITICAL

Brotherstone, T. (ed.), *Covenant, Charter, and Party* (Aberdeen, 1989).
Cameron, K. J., 'William Weir and the origins of the "Manchester League" in Scotland, 1833–39', *SHR*, lviii (1979).
Devine, T. M. (ed.), *Conflict and Stability in Scottish Society 1700–1850* (Edinburgh, 1990).
Devine, T. M. *Scottish Elites* (Edinburgh, 1994).
Dyer, M., *Men of Property and Intelligence. The Scottish Electoral System Prior to 1884* (Aberdeen, 1996).
Dyer, M., *Capable Citizens and Improvident Democrats. The Scottish Electoral System 1884–1929* (Aberdeen, 1996).

Finlay, R. J., *A Partnership for Good? Scottish Politics and the Union Since 1880* (Edinburgh, 1997).
Finlay, R. J., 'Scotland in the twentieth century: in defence of oligarchy?', *SHR*, lxxiii (1994).
Fraser, W. H., *Conflict and Class. Scottish Workers 1700–1838* (Edinburgh, 1988).
Fry, M., *Patronage and Principle. A Political History of Modern Scotland* (Aberdeen, 1987).
Gibson, J. S., *The Thistle and the Crown. A History of the Scottish Office* (Edinburgh, 1985).
Hanham, H. J., *Scottish Nationalism* (London, 1969).
Harvie, C., *Scotland and Nationalism. Scottish Society and Politics, 1707–1977* (2nd edn, London, 1994).
Hutchison, I. G. C., *A Political History of Scotland 1832–1924* (Edinburgh, 1986).
Kellas, J. G., *Modern Scotland* (rev. edn, London, 1980).
Knox, W., *Scottish Labour Leaders 1918–1939* (Edinburgh, 1984).
Lynch, M., *Scotland, 1850–1979: Society, Politics and the Union* (Historical Association Committee for Scotland and the Historical Association, 1994).
MacDougall, I. (ed.), *Essays in Scottish Labour History* (Edinburgh, 1978).
Mitchell, J., *Conservatives and the Union* (Edinburgh, 1990).
Morris, R. J. and Morton, G., 'Where was nineteenth-century Scotland?', *SHR*, lxxiii (1994).
Walker, W. M., *Juteopolis. Dundee and its Textile Workers 1885–1923* (Edinburgh, 1979).
Wilson, A., *The Chartist Movement in Scotland* (Manchester, 1970).
Wilson, G. M., *Alexander McDonald. Leader of the Miners* (Aberdeen, 1982).

CULTURAL

Anderson, R. D., *Education and the Scottish People 1750–1918* (Oxford, 1995).
Ash, M., *The Strange Death of Scottish History* (Edinburgh, 1980).
Bell, A. (ed.), *Lord Cockburn. A Bicentenary Commemoration* (Edinburgh, 1979).
Brown, C. G., *The People in the Pews* (The Economic and Social History Society of Scotland, 1993).
Brown, C. G., *The Social History of Religion in Scotland Since 1730* (London, 1987).
Brown, S. J., *Thomas Chalmers and the Godly Commonwealth* (Oxford, 1982).
Cheyne, A. C., *The Transforming of the Kirk. Victorian Scotland's Religious Revolution* (Edinburgh, 1983).
Donaldson, W., *Popular Literature in Victorian Scotland* (Aberdeen, 1986).
Drummond, A. L. and Bulloch, J., *The Scottish Church 1688–1843* (Edinburgh, 1973).
Drummond, A. L. and Bulloch, J., *The Church in Victorian Scotland 1843–1874* (Edinburgh, 1975).
Drummond, A. L. and Bulloch, J., *The Church in late Victorian Scotland 1874–1900* (Edinburgh, 1978).

Gifford, D., *The History of Scottish Literature. Volume 3. Nineteenth Century* (Aberdeen, 1988).

Hoeveler, J. D., *James McCosh and the Scottish Intellectual Tradition* (Princeton, 1981).

Humes, W. M. and Paterson, H. M. (eds), *Scottish Culture and Scottish Education 1800–1980* (Edinburgh, 1983).

Kidd, C., *Subverting Scotland's Past* (Cambridge, 1993).

McCrone, D., *Understanding Scotland. The Sociology of a Stateless Nation* (London, 1992).

McRoberts, D. (ed.), *Modern Scottish Catholicism 1878–1978* (Glasgow, 1979) (first published in the *Innes Review*, xix, 1978).

Robbins, K. *Nineteenth-century Britain. Integration and Diversity* (Oxford, 1988).

## SOCIAL AND ECONOMIC

Campbell, A. B., *The Lanarkshire Miners. A Social History of their Trade Unions, 1775–1874* (Edinburgh, 1979).

Campbell, R. H., *The Rise and Fall of Scottish Industry 1707–1939* (Edinburgh, 1980).

Devine, T. M., *Clanship to Crofters' War* (Manchester, 1994).

Devine, T. M. (ed.), *Farm Servants and Labour in Lowland Scotland 1770–1914* (Edinburgh, 1984).

Devine, T. M., *The Great Highland Famine* (Edinburgh, 1988).

Devine, T. M. and Jackson, G. (eds), *Glasgow Volume I: Beginnings to 1830* (Manchester, 1995).

Fraser, W. H. and Maver, I. (eds), *Glasgow Volume II: 1830 to 1912* (Manchester, 1996).

Devine, T. M. and Mitchison, R. (eds), *People and Society in Scotland I 1760–1830* (Edinburgh, 1988).

Fraser, W. H. and Morris, R. J. (eds), *People and Society in Scotland II 1830–1914* (Edinburgh, 1990).

Hunter, J., *The Making of the Crofting Community* (Edinburgh, 1976).

Lenman, B., *An Economic History of Modern Scotland* (London, 1977).

Moss, M. S. and Hume, J. R., *Workshop of the British Empire* (London, 1977).

Murray, N., *The Scottish Handloom Weavers 1790–1850: a Social History* (Edinburgh, 1978).

Parry, M. L. and Slater, T. R. (eds), *The Making of the Scottish Countryside* (London, 1980).

Slaven, A., *The Development of the West of Scotland 1750–1960* (London, 1975).

Slaven, A. and Checkland, S. (eds), *Dictionary of Scottish Business Biography*, 2 vols (Aberdeen, 1986, 1990).

Whittington, G. and Whyte, I. D. (eds), *An Historical Geography of Scotland* (London, 1983).

REFERENCE

Daiches, D. (ed.), *The New Companion to Scottish Culture* (rev. edn, Edinburgh, 1993).

Keay, J. and J., *Collins Encyclopaedia of Scotland* (London, 1994).

Thomson, D. S., *The Companion to Gaelic Scotland* (Oxford, 1983).

The two hundredth issue of the *Scottish Historical Review* (LXXV, 1996) contains a useful supplement that lists all of its articles and book reviews to date.

# INDEX